RE-ENGINEERING UNDER EXPLORED RENEWABLE ENERGY

Concepts and applications of renewable energies in Africa

BLESSING BARNET CHINIKO

Mwanaka Media and Publishing Pvt Ltd,
Chitungwiza Zimbabwe
*
Creativity, Wisdom and Beauty

Publisher: *Mmap*
Mwanaka Media and Publishing Pvt Ltd
24 Svosve Road, Zengeza 1
Chitungwiza Zimbabwe

mwanaka@yahoo.com
mwanaka13@gmail.com
https://www.mmapublishing.org
www.africanbookscollective.com/publishers/mwanaka-media-and-publishing
https://facebook.com/MwanakaMediaAndPublishing/

Distributed in and outside N. America by African Books Collective
orders@africanbookscollective.com
www.africanbookscollective.com

ISBN: 978-1-77934-080-1
EAN: 9781779340801

DISCLAIMER

All views expressed in this publication are those of the author and do not necessarily reflect the views of *Mmap.*

TABLE OF CONTENTS

BIOGAS

1.0 CONCEPT OF BIOGAS AND APPLICATIONS

Biogas can be produced from a variety of organic matter such as animal manures, human sewage, plant materials, food scraps, greases, and cellulose in food processing waste. In principle, biogas can be produced from any organic material. However, the organic material should not be rich in lignin as this compound is difficult to degrade by the anaerobic microorganisms. The process needs to be conducted at a controlled temperature (optimum around 37°C), around neutral pH, and under anaerobic conditions (Hossain et al.2022). Digester operators control parameters like temperature, acidity, alkalinity, and the carbon-to-nitrogen ratio to maximize gas production (Nandi et al., 2020). Digester designs vary with the operating temperature, different technologies, and different kinds of feedstock. It requires constant monitoring and proper operation, as oxygen and unwanted local microorganisms can be harmful to the digester and hinder the biogas/organic fertilizer production.

Biogas is a renewable, environmentally friendly energy source. It is produced by the bioconversion of decomposing organic matter through anaerobic digestion. Anaerobic digestion is a process in which natural microorganisms break down organic matter in the absence of air (Kirk & Gould, 2020). This process takes place in a sealed container known as a digester. The gas produced is mainly methane, with some carbon dioxide and other trace gases. It can be used as a fuel.

1.1. Definition and Composition

The biogas composition depends on the biomass, temperature, the microflora in the digester, pH, and residence time of the system. After anaerobic digestion, another vital product is digestate, which is a nutrient-rich fertilizer that we can use in agriculture. Therefore, anaerobic digestion has many advantages, such as converting waste into energy and recovering nutrients in the digestate for use on farms. However, the main challenges described concerning the anaerobic digestion process are the digester designs, mixing, the size and hotter temperature operation, efficient biogas use, contaminated residues with heavy metals, drugs, and micro-pollutants from domestic and industrial sources that present risks to the anaerobic methanogenic activity (Venegas et al.2021). This review highlights the different advances in both high-rate systems such as the anaerobic fixed-bed biofilm system and the hybrid systems such as the integrating with the photosynthetic reactors, challenges, and biogas use, through different models, a portable biogas system, wastes to be converted, movement sensors for biogas use control and abatement of the organic components toxic to the environment and humans.

Organic waste is a complex and heterogeneous mixture generally disposed in the environment, especially in landfills. The proper management of organic solid waste in the form of municipal solid waste is a critical factor for the preservation of life on the planet. In particular, anaerobic digestion has been shown to be an excellent option of valorization for one such material, and the amount of it is large, and has a positive energy balance, as well as new opportunities in energy generation through innovative biogas applications. Biogas is a biofuel that is obtained from the anaerobic digestion of organic matter such as agricultural residues, manure, sewage, municipal waste, plant material, and any organic matter in the absence of air. The anaerobic digestion of organic materials is a chemical process that produces a biogas composed mostly of methane, which is a renewable biological-based source of bioenergy. It is a process mediated by various groups of bacteria species that feed on waste materials, and the result is a useful combustible gas. Biogas is also an attractive alternative to landfill disposal because it allows the valorization of organic waste, reducing emissions of odors, greenhouse gases, and the leachate may also be reused in the field. Factors such as the choice of suitable feedstock, the operation of the reactor, the proper control of the process, the productive and economic issues, storage, and use of biogas will influence the quality and quantity of the formed biogas. It mainly consists of methane (CH_4) (50-75%) and carbon dioxide (CO_2) (25-50%), with tiny amounts of sulfur-containing compounds that are responsible for a bad smell.

Biogas is a biofuel that is a result of the anaerobic digestion of organic matter such as manure, sewage, municipal waste, plant material, and any other organic matter, in the absence of oxygen. Through natural processes, different biogases are produced that differ in proportion of methane, carbon dioxide, and other trace gases (Wu et al.2021). These are produced in the following ranges of percent by volume: methane (CH_4) (50-75%), carbon dioxide (CO_2) (25-50%), nitrogen (N_2) (2-30%), hydrogen sulfide (H_2S) (0-3%). The non-polluting use of biofuels is one of the best ways to contribute to reducing climate change derived from energy consumption. Biogas can be used as a fuel in a combustion engine, a microturbine, or utilized in engines or in fuel cells. In addition to the renewable source of the organic material through the biogas, due to its composition, it can be used in many different applications such as in the kitchens as a source for washing, transportation, cogeneration to produce heat and electricity, and even injection in the natural gas grid. Biogas systems produce not only biogas but also digestate which is a nutrient-rich fertilizer that can be used in agriculture.

1.1.1 Energy Sustainability Challenges

Restaurants in high density suburbs of Zimbabwe often rely on wood as a cooking fuel due to its affordability and accessibility. However, cooking with wood can have detrimental effects on both the environment and human health.

Figure 1: Restaurants in High density suburbs of Zimbabwe using wood

One of the major health concerns associated with cooking using wood is indoor air pollution. Wood combustion releases high levels of particulate matter and toxic gases such as carbon monoxide and nitrogen dioxide. In poorly ventilated kitchens, these pollutants can accumulate and pose serious risks to the health of restaurant workers and customers, leading to respiratory problems, eye irritation, and even lung diseases.

Furthermore, burning wood for cooking contributes to deforestation and environmental degradation.

Zimbabwe, like many other African countries, has been experiencing significant deforestation rates due to the increasing demand for firewood. Deforestation not only leads to the loss of biodiversity but also exacerbates climate change and decreases the availability of wood resources for future generations. Energy poverty is a pressing issue in Zimbabwe, where a large portion of the population lacks access to modern and reliable energy sources. According to the World Bank, over 60% of households in Zimbabwe rely on traditional biomass, including wood, for cooking. This high dependence on wood as a cooking fuel is a reflection of energy poverty, as it limits economic activities and hampers social development.

Figure 2: Increased Deforestation supplying wood to major urban areas in Zimbabwe

The increased deforestation in Zimbabwe to supply wood to major urban areas is driven by the high energy demand for cooking and heating purposes. As mentioned earlier, a significant portion of the population in Zimbabwe lacks access to modern and reliable energy sources, leading to a heavy reliance on traditional biomass, primarily wood. Urban areas, with their higher population density, have a much greater demand for energy compared to rural areas. This is due to the larger number of households, commercial establishments such as restaurants, and industries in urban centers. As a result, the demand for firewood in these areas is particularly high, leading to increased deforestation.

One practical example of this energy demand and its impact on deforestation can be seen in the capital city of Zimbabwe, Harare. With a population of over two million people, Harare's urban areas have a substantial need for cooking fuel. Many low-income households rely on wood as a cheap source of energy, leading to the unsustainable extraction of firewood from nearby forests. In addition to the domestic sector, the restaurant industry in major urban areas also contributes to the high energy demand for cooking. Restaurants typically require large volumes of firewood to meet their cooking needs, especially those that serve traditional and wood-fired cuisine. As a result, they contribute significantly to the deforestation in Zimbabwe. To address this issue, initiatives have been implemented to promote alternative cooking solutions and reduce the demand for firewood. One such initiative is the introduction of energy-efficient stoves in urban areas, which require less wood for cooking. These stoves are designed to maximize fuel efficiency and reduce emissions, helping to minimize the environmental impact of cooking.

Another practical example is the use of solar energy for cooking in urban areas. The falling costs of solar technologies, coupled with government incentives, have led to an increasing adoption of solar cookers in Zimbabwe. These cookers use sunlight to generate heat for cooking, eliminating the need for firewood altogether. Solar cooking not only reduces deforestation but also contributes to a cleaner and more sustainable energy system.

Figure 3: Poor environmental waste management practices

Poor environmental waste management practices in major urban areas of Zimbabwe have led to significant challenges in handling waste and its potential for converting waste into energy. The lack of proper waste management systems, including insufficient collection, inadequate disposal facilities, and limited recycling initiatives, has resulted in the accumulation of waste in urban areas. The waste volume statistics generated by poor waste management practices in Zimbabwe's major urban areas are alarming. According to the Ministry of Environment, Climate, Tourism, and Hospitality Industry, Harare, the capital city, produces approximately 1,600 tons of waste per day. However, the waste collection system can only handle around 600 tons per day, leaving a significant portion of the waste uncollected and causing it to accumulate on streets and in open spaces.

The situation is similar in other major urban areas such as Bulawayo, Mutare, and Gweru. These cities generate significant amounts of waste, with Bulawayo producing around 750 tons per day, Mutare producing around 150 tons per day, and Gweru producing around 250 tons per day. However, the waste management infrastructure in these cities is inadequate to handle these volumes effectively. The poor waste management practices also extend to the disposal of waste. The majority of urban areas in

Zimbabwe lack proper landfill sites, and as a result, open dumping and burning of waste are commonly practiced. This not only creates an eyesore and poses health risks but also contributes to air and soil pollution. The burning of waste releases harmful pollutants into the atmosphere, worsening air quality and impacting public health.

Moreover, the lack of adequate recycling initiatives exacerbates the waste management problem in urban areas. The majority of waste generated in Zimbabwe is not properly sorted and recycled, leading to valuable resources and energy potential being lost. Proper recycling systems and facilities are limited in urban areas, further contributing to the accumulation of waste and the missed opportunity for waste-to-energy conversion. However, there is potential for turning waste into energy in Zimbabwe's major urban areas. Waste-to-energy technologies, such as anaerobic digestion and incineration, can be utilized to convert organic waste into biogas or electricity. These technologies have the potential to address the energy demand in urban areas while also reducing the volume of waste that needs to be disposed of.

1.1.3 MONOPOLY OF LPG GAS IN ZIMBABWE

Figure 4: Monopoly of LPG Gas in Zimbabwe.

The monopoly of LPG gas in Zimbabwe has had a significant impact on equitable energy access, particularly for low-income households and communities. The monopolistic company that controls the import, distribution, and pricing of LPG gas has unjustifiably increased prices, making the fuel unaffordable for many

Zimbabwean households. One example of unjustified LPG gas increases is the sudden price hikes without proper justification or transparency. The monopolistic company has been known to raise prices arbitrarily, without any clear explanation as to why such increases are necessary. This lack of transparency has eroded trust and made it difficult for consumers to understand or plan for the rising costs of LPG gas. The effects of these price increases on energy poverty in Zimbabwe are profound. Many households, especially those living in poverty, are unable to afford LPG gas for cooking or heating purposes. As a result, they are forced to rely on more traditional and often inefficient energy sources, such as firewood or charcoal. These alternatives not only contribute to deforestation but also pose health risks due to indoor air pollution. The lack of affordable, clean, and reliable energy options perpetuates the cycle of energy poverty, making it difficult for vulnerable communities to improve their living conditions.

Furthermore, the of LPG gas in the energy market has hampers competition and limits innovation in the energy mix of Zimbabwe. In terms of the trends of LPG gas increases, there has been a consistent pattern of price hikes over the years. For example, in 2019, the price of a 5-kg cylinder of LPG gas increased by more than

50% within a few months, making it even more unaffordable for households.

1.1.4 POWER CHALLENGES IN SOUTHERN AFRICA AND ITS EFFECTS ON ECONOMIC ACTVITIES.

In South Africa, the overreliance on coal-generated power has been a significant challenge impacting economic activities. The country's state-owned utility, Eskom, has been struggling with aging coal-fired power plants, leading to frequent power outages and load shedding. These power cuts have had detrimental effects on various industries, such as mining, manufacturing, and agriculture. For instance, during the 2019 energy crisis, mining operations were disrupted, causing production losses and financial setbacks. In addition, businesses had to incur additional costs for alternative power sources, such as diesel generators, to maintain operations during power cuts.

Figure 5: Electricity Crisis in Southern Africa.

Zimbabwe has also been experiencing electricity challenges due to its dependence on coal-generated power and the limited capacity of its aging infrastructure. The country has faced prolonged power cuts, with businesses and households enduring hours of load shedding. These outages have had severe consequences for industries like manufacturing, where production schedules have been disrupted, leading to reduced output and revenue losses. For example, the manufacturing sector in Zimbabwe recorded a 13% decline in output in 2019 due to power shortages, according to the Confederation of Zimbabwe Industries.

In Malawi, the electricity sector has been struggling with high energy tariffs, unreliable power supply, and limited access to electricity in rural areas. The country predominantly relies on hydroelectric power, but challenges such as erratic weather patterns and climate change have affected power generation. This has had adverse effects on businesses, particularly in the agro-processing and textile industries. Reduced access to electricity and unreliable power supply have hampered production processes, delaying deliveries and incurring extra costs for businesses.

Zambia, known for its hydroelectric potential, has faced challenges in its electricity sector due to dependence on hydropower and the vulnerability to droughts. The country's reliance on coal-fired power plants as a backup has raised concerns about environmental impacts and sustainability. For businesses in sectors like tourism and hospitality, power shortages have resulted in disruptions to services, affecting customer satisfaction and revenue. For instance, hotels and lodges have had to resort to expensive alternative power sources during outages, impacting their operational costs and profitability.

The overreliance on coal-generated power in these countries not only hinders economic activities but also exacerbates environmental issues such as air pollution, greenhouse gas emissions, and water contamination. Transitioning to renewable energy sources like solar, wind, and hydro power is crucial to addressing the electricity challenges in Southern Africa and achieving sustainable development. By diversifying the energy mix and investing in clean energy technologies.

1.2 PORTABLE BIOGAS SYSTEMS

1.2.1 Portable Biogas Systems Applicability in Kenya.

The usage of homebiogas systems in Kenyan hospitals has gained significant popularity in recent years. These systems are composed of an anaerobic digester, which converts organic waste into biogas and a biofertilizer. The organic waste typically includes kitchen waste, sewage, agricultural waste, and cow dung.

Figure 6 Homebiogas system

In hospitals, these systems are commonly used to generate renewable energy for cooking, heating, and electricity generation. The biogas produced can be used in gas stoves, ovens, boilers, and even in generators to provide uninterrupted power supply. This not only reduces reliance on fossil fuels but also helps in cost savings for the hospitals. One of the key advantages of using homebiogas systems in hospitals is the reduction of waste management costs. Hospitals generate a significant amount of organic waste on a daily basis, and disposing of this waste can be a costly affair. By using a homebiogas system, hospitals can convert this waste into biogas, which can be used for their energy needs.

Additionally, the organic waste is also converted into a nutrient-rich biofertilizer that can be used for gardening or agriculture, effectively closing the waste loop.

Another advantage is the reduced environmental impact. By utilizing organic waste for biogas production, hospitals can reduce their greenhouse gas emissions and contribute to reducing carbon footprints. This aligns with global sustainability goals and promotes a more eco-friendly and sustainable healthcare system in Kenya. In terms of technical requirements, homebiogas systems require a certain amount of space for installation. A designated area for waste collection and digestion, as well as storage tanks for biogas and biofertilizer, are necessary. The systems also require regular monitoring and maintenance to ensure optimal performance and prevent any issues.

A practical example of the usage of homebiogas systems in Kenyan hospitals can be observed in Nakuru County Referral Hospital. The hospital implemented a homebiogas system to manage its organic waste and generate biogas for cooking and electricity. By utilizing the waste produced in the hospital kitchen and other organic waste from the hospital premises, the system has significantly reduced the hospital's reliance on fossil fuels and has saved costs on energy bills.

In conclusion, the usage of homebiogas systems in Kenyan hospitals offers a sustainable and cost-effective solution for waste management and energy generation. With the ability to convert organic waste into renewable energy and biofertilizer, these systems provide numerous advantages, including cost savings, reduced environmental impact.

1.3 PORTABLE BIOGAS FOR HOME USE IN SOUTH AFRICA

Portable home biogas systems are gaining popularity in South Africa as a sustainable and efficient solution for household waste management and energy generation. These systems typically consist of a small-scale anaerobic digester that can convert organic waste into biogas and biofertilizer in a compact and portable design. The organic waste commonly used in these systems includes food scraps, kitchen waste, sewage, and animal manure.

Figure 7: Portable biogas system.

The main usage of portable home biogas systems is for cooking and heating purposes. The biogas produced can be utilized in gas stoves and ovens to replace traditional fossil fuels such as coal or wood. This not only reduces reliance on non-renewable energy sources but also decreases indoor air pollution and improves overall household air quality. One of the key advantages of using portable home biogas systems is the reduction of waste and its associated disposal costs. South African households generate a significant amount of organic waste that is typically disposed of in landfills. By implementing a biogas system, households can convert this waste into a useful resource while reducing the environmental impact.

Additionally, portable home biogas systems provide an alternative energy source for remote or off-grid areas. Many rural communities in South Africa do not have access to reliable electricity, making it challenging for them to meet their basic household energy needs. By utilizing biogas systems, these communities can generate their own renewable energy and improve their living conditions.

In terms of technical requirements, portable home biogas systems require a small amount of space for installation. The size of the digester determines the capacity and efficiency of the system. The systems typically consist of an inlet for the organic waste, an anaerobic digestion chamber, and an outlet for biogas collection. Some systems also include a biofertilizer storage tank for the processed waste. A practical example of the usage of portable home biogas systems in South Africa can be seen in the rural village of Mahikeng. The local community implemented portable biogas systems to manage their organic waste and generate cooking gas for their households. By utilizing food waste and cow dung, these households have reduced their reliance on traditional cooking fuels and improved their energy security.

In conclusion, portable home biogas systems in South Africa provide a sustainable and cost-effective solution for waste management and energy generation. With the ability to convert organic waste into renewable biogas and biofertilizer, these systems offer numerous advantages, including reduced waste disposal costs, alternative energy sources, and improved.

1.4 Balloon Plants

Biogas balloon plants, also known as biogas digesters, are a technology used to convert organic waste materials, such as agricultural residue, food waste, and animal manure, into biogas through a process called anaerobic digestion. These biogas plants are mostly applicable in rural areas with agricultural activities and livestock farming, where there is a significant production of organic waste. They provide a sustainable solution to both waste management and energy needs in countries like South Africa and Zambia.

In South Africa, biogas balloon plants have been implemented in agricultural farms and communities to tackle the issue of waste management and energy poverty. One example is the Thabazimbi Biogas Project in Limpopo province. This project utilizes cattle manure from a local feedlot and organic waste from a nearby town as feedstock for the biogas digester. The waste materials are fed into a sealed container, where anaerobic bacteria break them down and produce biogas. The biogas is then captured and stored in a balloon or gas holder. The biogas produced from these balloon plants can be used for various purposes, including cooking, heating, and electricity generation. In the Thabazimbi Biogas Project, the biogas is used to generate electricity, which is then utilized on the farm and supplied to the local grid, providing a sustainable energy source for the community.

At South Africa's most northern air force base, on the outskirts of Louis Trichardt in Limpopo, a biodigester has been successfully producing biogas for the past two years, as part of a pilot project with the South African National Energy Development Institute (SANEDI). Precast biodigesters were installed at Air Force Base Makhado and the 523 Squadron (SQN) army base, which were selected as the pilot sites for the Department of Defence's biodigester project to turn kitchen food waste destined for landfill into biogas for cooking.

Biodigester pilot project at Limpopo military bases a success

The biogas plants consist of large, sealed anaerobic digesters in which waste material is decomposed to produce methane gas. These were installed underground at the bases to make them unobtrusive and to prevent any unpleasant sights or smells around them. In addition to gas for cooking, the digesters produce an organic by-product, called the digestate, which is an excellent organic fertiliser. The upshot of the digester's happiness is that it produces enough gas for the stove-top cooking required to provide breakfast and supper for 220 people every day, thus saving a predicted amount of about 116 MWh of electricity over the combined system's lifetime. Based on this performance, it will be possible to add two more biodigesters in parallel on this system to power additional cooking burners and a water heater in the kitchen.

The pilot at the 523 SQN base has followed a more roundabout route to success. Although the base commander had also adopted his biodigester from the start, the duties of a high-ranking officer limited the attention he could pay to it. The biodigester has needed "resuscitation" twice since July 2021– both times the commanding officer had been away from base. Surridge laughs at the memory of receiving a phone call on a Saturday morning: "Doctor, the baby is dead!" shouted the officer down the line. It seemed that cleaning fluids used to clean the sink in which the macerator is installed had ended up in the biodigester and instantly killed all the bacteria.

There was also the time when the system was fed too much undiluted starch, which clogged the pipes and the resultant gas build-up blew back into the kitchen through the sink. "It looked like the macerator had vomited," says Surridge. Although it has taken almost 21 months to reach full capacity, 523's biodigester is humming these days, producing enough cooking gas to prepare daily meals for the people stationed at the base. To date, 17.5 MWh of electricity has been saved, 6.5 t of carbon dioxide emissions eliminated and 30 t of kitchen waste diverted from landfill. The two bases were carefully chosen to demonstrate that biodigester plants can be tailored to specific needs and provide a wide range of solutions, and that they can be scaled up or down by order of magnitude, depending on the energy requirements and raw materials available.

Another practical example of biogas balloon plants can be found in Zambia. The Chongwe Dairy Biogas Project is an initiative that aims to address waste management challenges and energy poverty in the dairy farming sector. The project utilizes cow manure from dairy farms to produce biogas through anaerobic digestion. The biogas is then used for cooking and heating purposes, reducing the reliance on traditional fuels like firewood and charcoal.

Biogas comes in handy
SNV helping to promote alternative clean energy across Zambia

A BIO digester plant provided by SNV in in Silver Nyadebi's backyard.

The implementation of biogas balloon plants in South Africa and Zambia provides multiple benefits. Firstly, it addresses the waste management problem by converting organic waste into biogas, effectively reducing methane emissions, which is a potent greenhouse gas. Secondly, it provides a renewable and sustainable source of energy, reducing the dependence on fossil fuels and mitigating environmental pollution. Additionally, it contributes to rural electrification, improving access to clean energy in remote areas.

1.5 TECHNICAL ASPECT OF THE BIO GAS PLANTS

The balloon plant consists of a digester bag (e.g., PVC) in the upper part in which the gas is stored. The inlet and outlet are attached directly to the plastic skin of the balloon. The gas pressure is achieved through the elasticity of the balloon and by added weights placed on the balloon. The advantages of this system are its low cost, ease of transportation, low construction sophistication, high digester temperatures, and its rather simple cleaning, emptying and maintenance. The disadvantages can be the relatively short life span, high susceptibility to damage, little creation of local employment and, therefore, limited self-help potential. A variation of the balloon plant is the channel-type digester, which is usually covered with plastic sheeting and a sunshade. Balloon plants can be recommended wherever the balloon skin is not likely to be damaged and where temperatures are not too high.

Low Cost Flexible Bio gas Digester

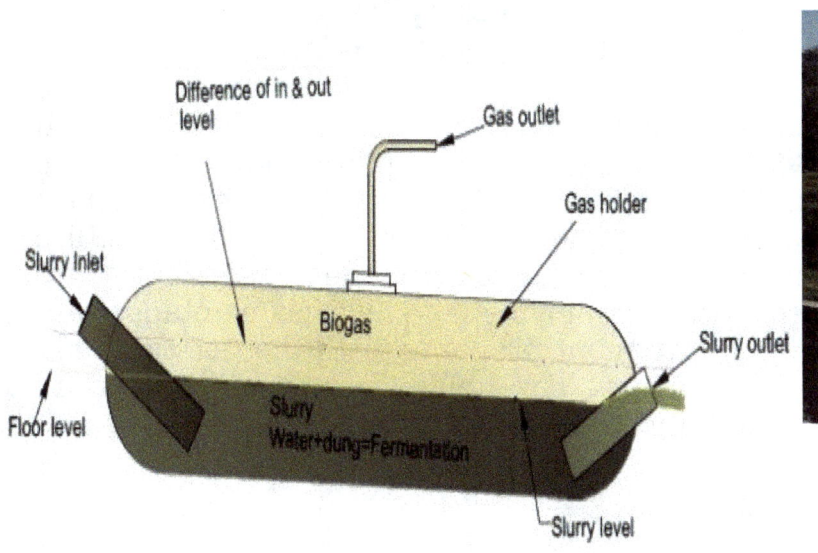

Figure 1:Balloon Biogas plant

1.6 Fixed-Dome Plants

The fixed-dome plant consists of a digester with a fixed, non-movable gas holder, which sits on top of the digester. When the production of gas starts, the slurry is displaced into the compensation tank. The gas pressure increases with the volume of gas stored and the height difference between the slurry level in the digester and the slurry level in the compensation tank. The advantages of this system

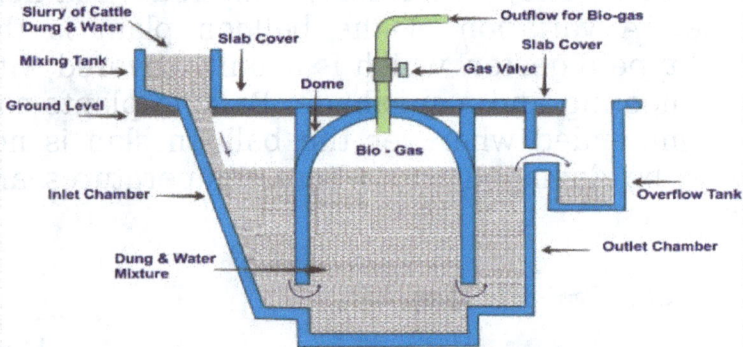

Fixed Dome type Bio-gas Plant

are the relatively low construction costs and the absence of moving parts and rusting steel parts. If well-constructed, fixed-dome plants have a long life span. The underground construction saves space and protects the digester from temperature changes. The construction provides opportunities for skilled local employment. The disadvantages are mainly the frequent problems with the gas-tightness of the brickwork gas holder, where even a small crack in the upper brickwork can cause a heavy loss of biogas. Therefore, fixed-dome plants are recommended only where construction can be supervised by experiencedbiogas technicians. The gas pressure fluctuates substantially depending on the volume of the stored gas. Even though the underground construction buffers temperature extremes, digester temperatures are low.

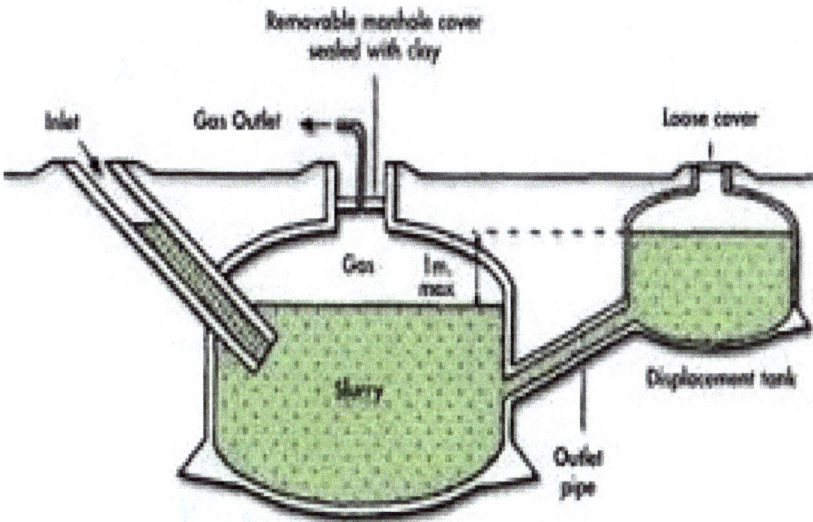

1.7 Floating-Drum Plants

Floating-drum plants consist of an underground digester and a moving gasholder. The gasholder floats either directly on the fermentation slurry or in a water jacket of its own. The gas is collected in the gas drum, which rises or moves down, according to the amount of gas stored. The gas drum is prevented from tilting by a guiding frame. If the drum floats in a water jacket, it cannot get stuck, even in substrate with a high solid content. The main advantage of this system is its simple, easy operation, as the volume of stored gas is directly visible to the user. The gas pressure is constant and determined by the weight of the gas holder. The construction is relatively easy and mistakes do not lead to major problems in operation or gas yield. The disadvantages are high material costs of the steel drum and the susceptibility of steel parts due to corrosion. Because of this, floating-drum plants have a shorter life span than fixed-dome plants and regular maintenance costs for the painting of the drum.

Figure 2:Floating Dome Biogas Digester

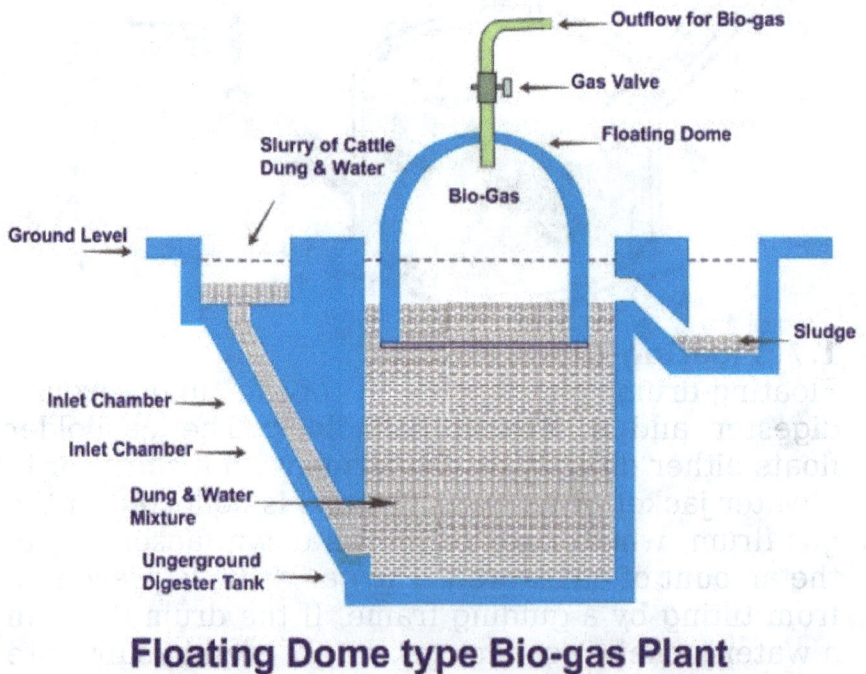

Floating Dome type Bio-gas Plant

1.8 Batch type biogas plant

Batch type biogas plants are appropriate where daily supplies of raw waste materials are difficult to be obtained. A batch loaded digester is filled to capacity sealed and given sufficient retention time in the digester. After completion of the digestion, the residue is emptied and filled again. Gas production is uneven because bacterial digestion starts slowly, peaks and then tapers off with growing consumption of volatile solids. The salient features of batch-fed type biogas plants are:

(i) Gas production in batch type is uneven.

(ii) Batch type plants may have several digesters for continuous supply of gas.

(iii) Several digesters occupy more space.

(iv) This type of plants require large volume of digester, therefore, initial cost becomes high.

(v) This plant needs addition of fermented slurry to start the digestion process.

1.9 Continous type biogass plant

In continuous type biogas plant, the supply of the gas is continuous and the digester is fed with biomass regularly. Continuous biogas plants may be single stage, double stage or multiple stage. Digestion of waste materials in a single chamber or digester is called single stage process, in two chambers or digester is called multi stage process. In double stage process, acidogenic and methanogenic stage are physically separated into two chambers. Thus, the first stage of acid

35

production is carried out in a separate chamber and only diluted acids are fed into the second chamber where biomethanation takes place.

In single stage,acidogenic and methanogenic stage are carried out in the same chamber without barrier. These plants are economic, simple and easy to operate. these plants are generally for small and medium size biogas plants. However,the two stage biogas plants are costlier, difficult in operation and maintenance but they produce more gas. These plants are preferred for larger biogas plant system. The important features of continous type biogas plants are:

(i) Gas production is continuous.
(ii) Retention period is less
(iii) Less problems as compared to batch type.
(iv) Small digestion chambers are required

2.0 APPLICATIONS OF BIO GAS IN THE COMMERCIAL SECTOR

2.1 Agricultural biogas plants

The agricultural biogas plants are considered those plants which are processing feedstock ofagricultural origin. The most common feedstock types for this kind of plants are animalmanure and slurries, vegetable residues and vegetable by products, dedicated energy crops(DEC), but also various residues from food and fishing industries etc. Animal manure andslurries, from cattle and pig production, are the basic feedstock for most agricultural biogasplants

Digestate is used as fertilizer on the farm and the surplus is sold to plant farms in the nearby area. The produced biogas by anaerobic digestion(AD) is used in a gas engine, for electricity and heat production using CHP. About 10 to 30% of the produced heat and electricity is used to operate the biogas plant and for domestic needs of the farmer, while the surplus is sold to power companies and respectively to neighboring heat consumers. Agricultural biogas plants are divided into three groups by electrical capacity of CHP unit: Small scale ≤ 70 kW , Medium scale 70-150 kW and Large scale 150-500 kW.

2.2 Waste water treatment plants

AD is largely used for treatment of primary and secondary sludge, resulted from aerobic treatment of municipal waste water. The system is applied in many countries in combination with advanced treatment systems where the AD process is used to stabilise and reduce the final amount of sludge. Most engineering companies providing sewage treatment systems have also the capability to provide AD systems. In European countries, between 30 and 70% of sewage sludge is treated by AD, depending on national legislation and priorities. The AD treated sludge effluent can be further used as fertiliser on agricultural land or for energy production by incineration.

2.3 Municipal solid waste (MSW) treatment plants

In many countries, municipal solid waste is collected as mixed stream and incinerated in large power plants or disposed on landfill sites. This practice is actually a waste of energy and nutrients, as most of the organic fraction could be source separated and used as AD feedstock. Even bulk collected wastes can be further processed and used for biogas production.

In recent years, source separation and recycling of wastes received increasing attention. As a result, separate fractions of MSW are now becoming available for more advanced recycling treatment, prior to disposal. The origin of the organic waste is important in determining which treatment method is most appropriate. Kitchen waste is generally too wet and lacks in structure for aerobic composting, but provides an excellent feedstock for AD. On the other hand, woody wastes contain high proportions of lignocellulosic material are better suited for composting, as pre-treatment is necessary in order to be used for AD.

Utilisation of source separated organic fraction of household waste for biogas production has a large potential and several hundred AD plants, processing organic fraction of MSW, are in operation around the world. The aim is to reduce the stream of organic wastes to landfills or even to incineration and to redirect them towards recycling.

2.4 Industrial biogas plants

Anaerobic processes are largely used for the treatment of industrial wastes and waste waters for more than a century and AD is today a standard technology for the treatment of various industrial waste waters from food-processing, agro-industries, and pharmaceutical industries. AD is also applied to pre-treat organic loaded industrial waste waters, before final disposal. Due to recent improvements of treatment technologies, diluted industrial waste waters can also be digested. Europe has a leading position in the world regarding this application of AD. In recent years energy considerations and environmental concerns have further increased the interest in direct anaerobic treatment of organic industrial wastes and the management of organic solid wastes from industry is increasingly controlled by environmental legislations.

Industries using AD for wastewater treatment range from: Food processes (vegetable canning, milk and cheese manufacture, slaughterhouses, potato processing industry), Beverage industry (breweries, soft drinks, distilleries, coffee, fruit juices), Industrial products (paper and board, rubber, chemicals, starch, pharmaceuticals)

Industrial biogas plants bring about a number of benefits for the society and the industries involved:

· Added value through nutrient recycling and cost reductions for disposal

· Utilisation of biogas to generate process energy

· Improved environmental image of the industries concerned, through environmental friendly treatment of the produced wastes.

It is expected that the environmental and socio-economic benefits of AD, complemented by higher costs/taxation of other disposal methods, will increase the number of applications of industrial biogas in the future.

2.5 Landfill gas recovery plants

Landfills can be considered as large anaerobic plants with the difference that the decomposition process is discontinuous and depends on the age of the landfill site. Landfill gas has a composition which is similar to biogas, but it can contain toxic gases, originating from decomposition of waste materials on the site. Recovery of landfill gas is not only essential for environmental protection and reduction of emissions of methane and other landfill gases but it is also a cheap source of energy, generating benefits through faster stabilisation of the landfill site and revenues from the gas utilisation. Due to the remoteness of landfill sites, landfill gas is normally used for electricity generation, but the full range of gas utilisation, from space heating to upgrading to vehicle fuel and pipeline quality is possible as well.

Landfill gas recovery can be optimised through the management of the site such as shredding the waste, re-circulating the organic fraction and treating the landfill as a bioreactor. A landfill bioreactor is a controlled landfill, designed to

40

accelerate the conversion of solid waste into methane and is typically divided into cells, provided with a system to collect leachate from the base of the cell. The collected leachate is pumped up to the surface and redistributed across the waste cells, transforming the landfill into a large high-solids digester

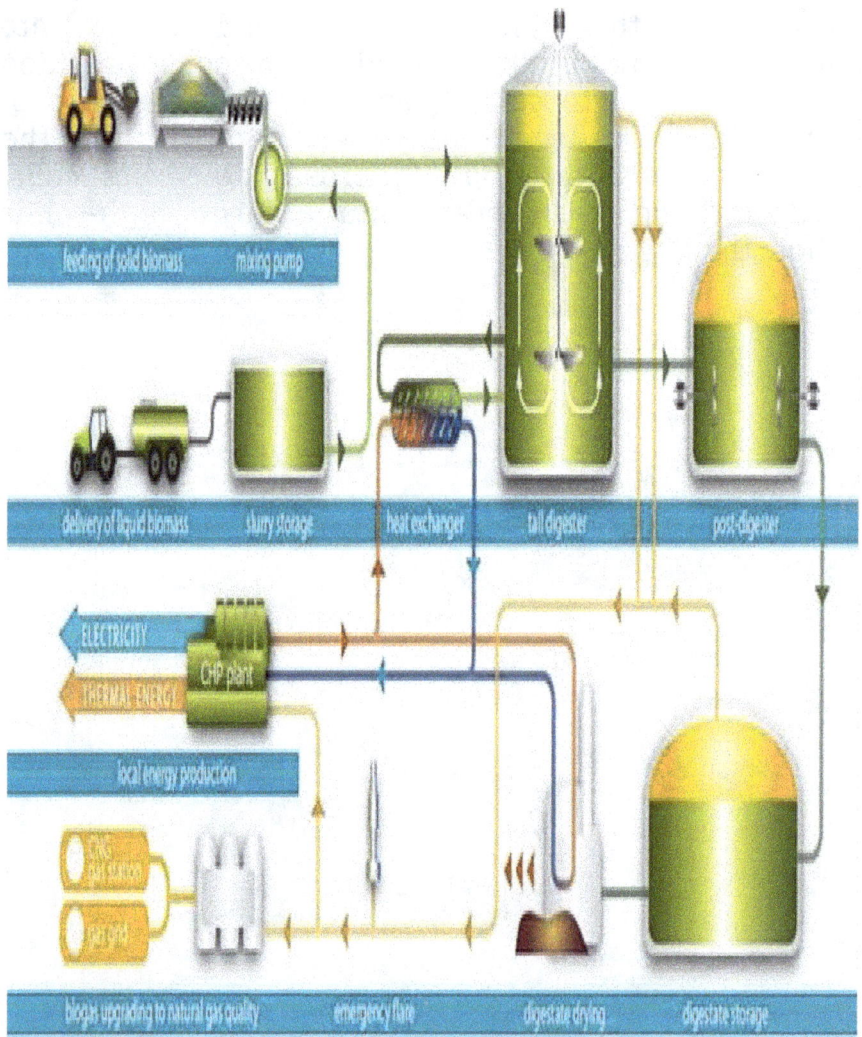

feeding of solid biomass   mixing pump

delivery of liquid biomass   slurry storage   heat exchanger   tail digester   post-digester

ELECTRICITY

THERMAL ENERGY

CHP plant

local energy production

CNG fuel station

gas grid

biogas upgrading to natural gas quality   emergency flare   digestate drying   digestate storage

42

3.0 ANAEROBIC DIGESTION PROCESS

Anaerobic digestion, or the decomposition of organic matter by bacteria in the absence of oxygen, occurs naturally in liquid manure systems. Biogas is produced by fermenting substrates with the exclusion of air to generate a combustible gas containing between 40% and 75% methane. The quantity of biogas generated depends on factors such as: temperature, residence time and the composition of the substrate in the fermenter. The complete biological decomposition of organic matter to methane and carbon dioxide under oxygen-depleted conditions is complicated and is an interaction between a number of different bacteria that are each responsible for their part of the task. What may be a waste product from some bacteria could be a substrate for others, and in this way the bacteria are interdependent.

The anaerobic decomposition of organic matter is often divided into three steps: Hydrolysis, acidogenesis and methanogenesis, where different groups of bacteria are each responsible for a step.

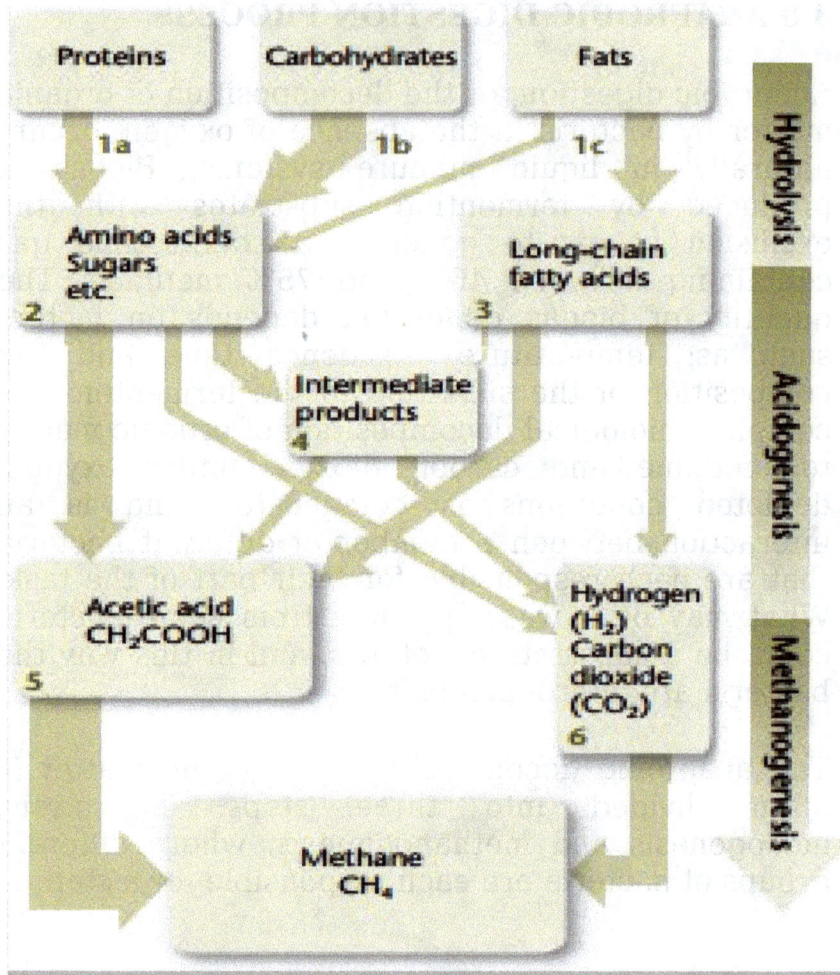

Figure 3:Processes of anaerobic digestion

3.1Hydrolysis
During hydrolysis long-chain molecules, such as

44

protein, carbohydrate and fat polymers, are broken down to monomers (small molecules). Here, liquefying bacteria convert insoluble, fibrous materials such as carbohydrates, fats and proteins into soluble substances. However, some fibrous material cannot be liquefied and can accumulate in the digester or can pass through the digester intact. Water and other inorganic material also can accumulate in the digester or pass through the digester unchanged. Undigested materials make up the low-odour, liquefied effluent.

3.2 Fermentation – Acidogenesis

Anaerobic digestion, acid-forming bacteria convert the soluble organic matter

(glucose, xylose, amino acids and fatty acids) into volatile acids. Twenty percent is converted to carbon dioxide and hydrogen (H2), while the remaining 30% is broken down into short-chain volatile fatty acids.

3.3 Methanogenesis

Methane- forming bacteria convert those volatile acids into biogas. Not all volatile acids and soluble organic compounds are converted to biogas; some become part of the effluent. Two different groups of bacteria are responsible for the methane production. One group degrades acetic acid to methane and the other produces methane from carbon dioxide and hydrogen. Under stable conditions, around 70% of the methane production comes from the degradation of acetic acid, while the remaining 30% comes from carbon dioxide and hydrogen. The two processes are finely balanced and inhibition of one will also lead to inhibition of the other. The methanogens have the slowest growth rate of the bacteria involved in the process, they also become the limiting factor for how quickly the process can proceed and how much material can be digested. The growth rate of the methanogens is only around one fifth of the acid-forming bacteria.

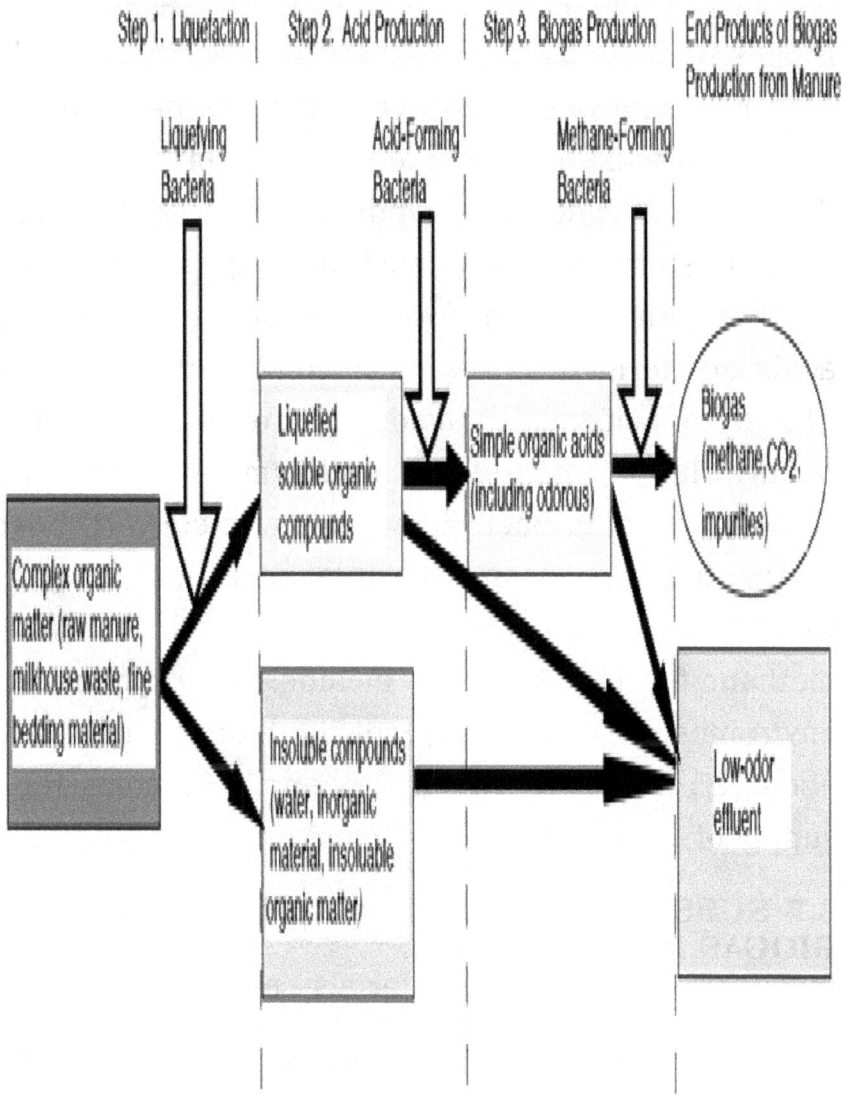

Figure 4:Methanogenesis process

Methane-forming bacteria are more sensitive to their environment than acid-forming bacteria. Acid-forming bacteria can survive under a wide range of conditions while methane-forming bacteria are more demanding. Under the conditions typical of liquid manure storages, more acid-forming bacteria can survive than methane- forming bacteria. Therefore, acids are formed and are not converted to biogas. This excess of volatile acids can result in a putrid odour. In a controlled, optimum environment, methane-forming bacteria survive and convert most of the odour-producing volatile acids into biogas. Conditions that encourage activity of both acid- and methane-forming bacteria include: An oxygen-free environment, A relatively constant temperature of about 95 °F, pH between 6.6 and 7.6, consistent supply of organic matter to "feed".

3.7 SUBSTRATE AND MATERIAL BALANCE OF BIOGAS PRODUCTION

In general, all organic materials can ferment or be digested. However, only homogenous and liquid substrates can be considered for simple biogas plants: faeces and urine from cattle, pigs and possibly poultry, as well as wastewater from toilets. When the plant is at capacity, the excrement is diluted with an equal quantity of liquid, such as urine if available. Waste and wastewater from food-processing industries are only suitable for simple plants if they are homogenous and in liquid forms. The maximum gas-production from a given amount of raw material depends on the type of substrate.

3.5 Composition and Properties of Biogas
Biogas is a mixture of gases mainly composed of:
➤ Methane (CH_4): 40-70 % by volume
➤ Carbon dioxide (CO_2): 30-60 % by volume
Other gases: 1-5 % by volume, including:
• Hydrogen (H_2): 0-1 % by volume
• Hydrogen sulfide (H_2S): 0-3 % by volume

Similar to any pure gas, the properties of biogas are pressure- and temperature-dependent. They are also affected by the moisture content and other major factors such as:change in volume as a function of temperature and pressure, change in calorific value as a function of temperature, pressure and water-vapor content and change in water-vapor content as a function of temperature and pressure. The calorific power of biogas is about 6 kWh/m3 - this corresponds to about half a litre of diesel oil.

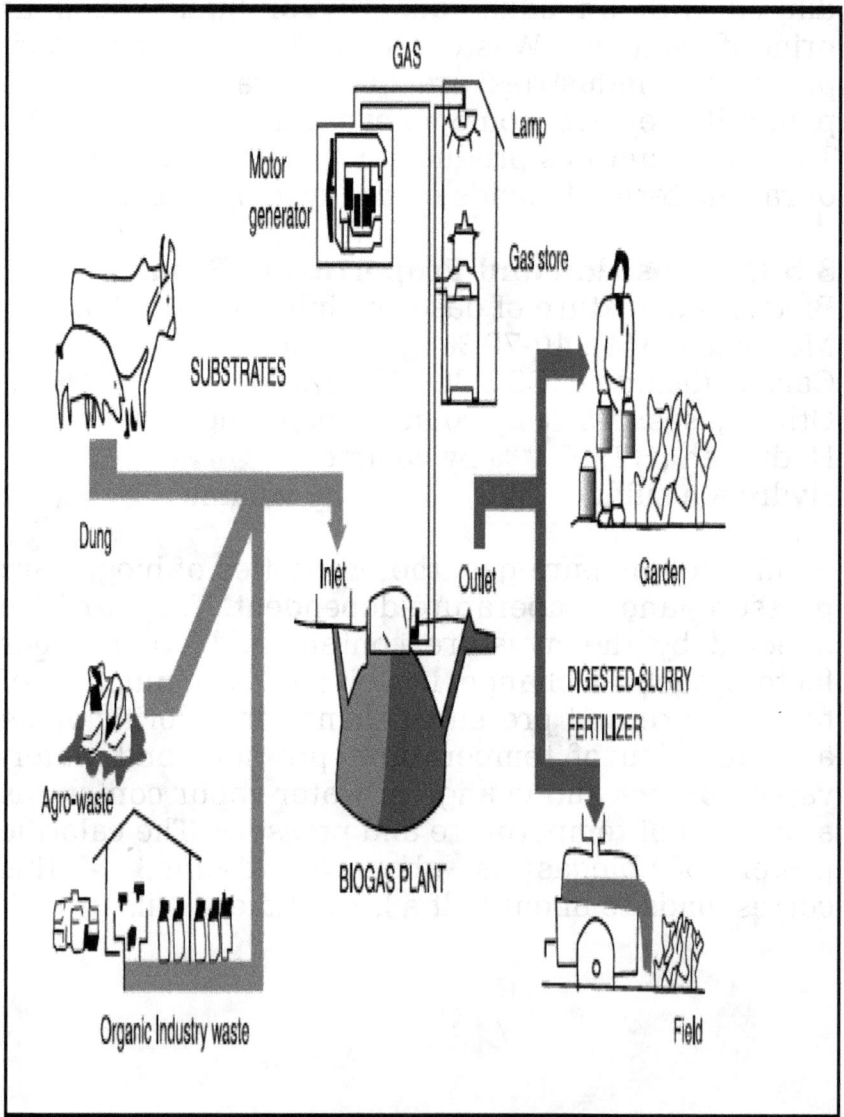

GAS

Motor generator

Lamp

Gas store

SUBSTRATES

Dung

Inlet

Outlet

Garden

DIGESTED-SLURRY
FERTILIZER

Agro-waste

BIOGAS PLANT

Organic Industry waste

Field

Figure 5:A typical biogas digester plant configuration

4.0 UTILISATION OF BIOGAS

Biogas has many energy utilisations, depending on the nature of the biogas source and the local demand. Generally, biogas can be used for heat production by direct combustion, electricity production by fuel cells or micro-turbines, CHP generation or as vehicle fuel.

7.1 Direct combustion and heat utilisation

The simplest way of utilising biogas is direct burning in boilers or burners, extensively used for the biogas produced by small family digesters. Direct combustion, in natural gas burners, is applied in many countries as well. Biogas can be burned for heat production either on site, or transported by pipeline to the end users. For heating purposes biogas does not need any upgrading, and the contamination level does not restrict the gas utilisation as much as in the case of other applications. However, biogas needs to undergo condensation and particulate removal, compression, cooling and drying.

7.20 Combined heat and power (CHP) generation

CHP generation is a standard utilisation of biogas from AD in many countries with a developed biogas sector, as it is considered a very efficient utilisation of biogas for energy production. Before CHP conversion, biogas is drained and dried. Most gas engines have maximum limits for the content of hydrogen sulphide, halogenated hydrocarbons and siloxanes in biogas. An engine based CHP power plant has an efficiency of up to 90% and produces 35% electricity and 65% heat. The most common types of CHP plants are block type thermal power plants (BTTP) with combustion motors that are coupled to a generator. Generators usually have a constant rotation of 1500 rpm (rotations per minute) in order to be compatible with the grid frequency. Motors can be Gas-Otto, Gas-Diesel or Gas-Pilot Injection engines. Both, Gas-diesel and Gas-Otto engines are operating without ignition oil, according to the Otto principle. The difference between these engines is only the compression. Thus, both motors will be referred to as Gas-Otto motors in the rest of the text. Alternatives to the above mentioned BTTPs are micro gas turbines, Stirling motors and fuel cells, all of them technologies undergoing important developmental steps during the recent years.

The produced electricity from biogas can be used as process energy for electrical equipment such as pumps, control systems and stirrers. In many countries with high feed-in tariffs for renewable electricity, all the produced electricity is sold to the grid and the process electricity is bought from the same national electricity grid.

7.30 Biogas micro-turbines

In biogas micro-turbines, air is pressed into a combustion chamber at high pressure and mixed with biogas. The air-biogas mixture is burned causing the temperature increase and the expanding of the gas mixture. The hot gases are released through a turbine, which is connected to the electricity generator (Figure 5.4). The electric capacity of micro-turbines is typically below 200 kWe. The cost of biogas micro-turbines is high and the research and development work in this area is therefore aiming cost reduction for future models.

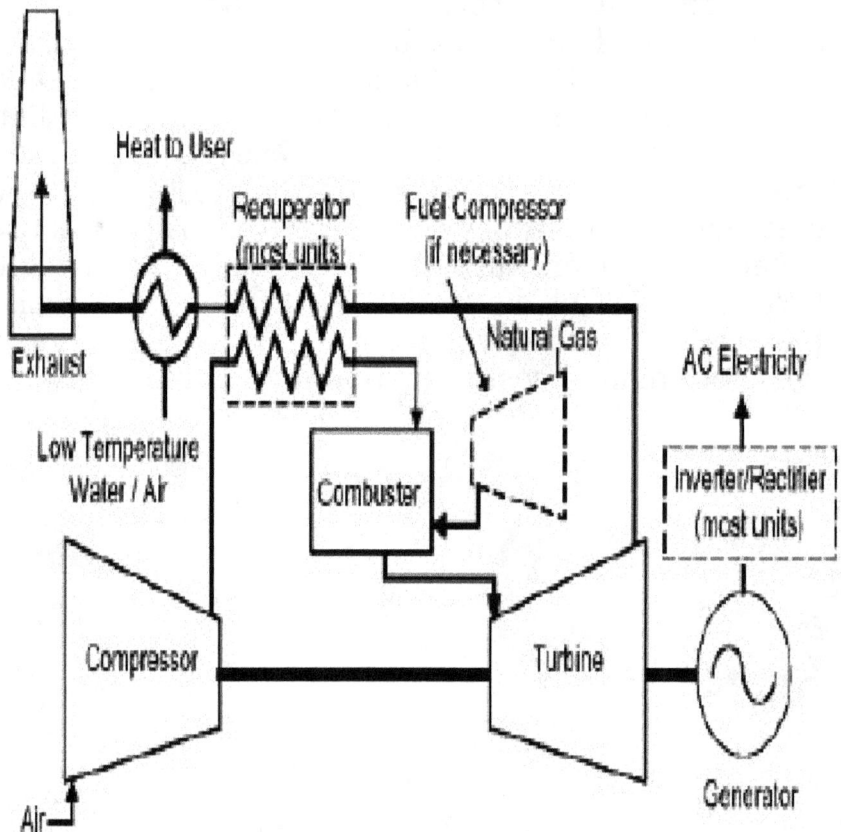

Figure 6:Micro-turbine structure

Source : www.energysolutionscenter.org

7.40 Fuel cells

The fuel cells are electrochemical devices that convert the chemical energy of a reaction directly into electrical energy. The basic physical structure (building block) of a fuel cell consists of an electrolyte layer in contact with a porous anode and cathode on both sides (Figure 5.5). In a typical fuel cell, the gaseous fuel (biogas) is fed continuously to the anode(the negative electrode) compartment and an oxidant (i.e. oxygen from air) is fed continuously to the cathode (the positive electrode) compartment. An electrochemical reaction takes place at the electrodes, producing electric current.

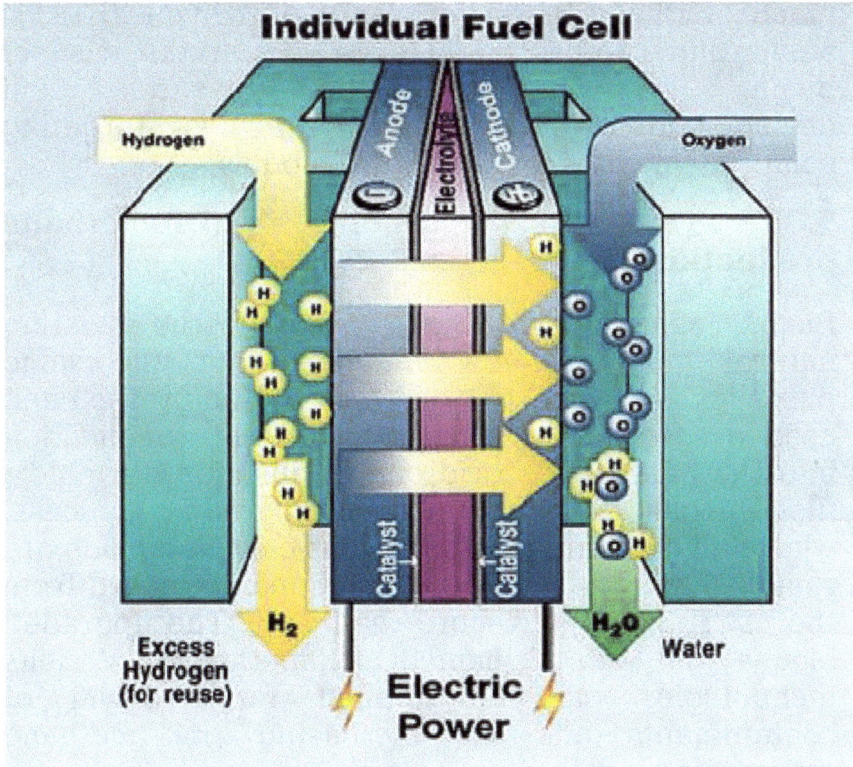

Figure 7:Simplified scheme of a fuel cell

Source: Emerging Environmental Issues, 2005

There are various fuel cell types suitable for biogas, named according to the type of electrolyte used. They can be low (AFC, Polymer-Electrolyte-Membrane *(PEM))*, medium (Phosphoric Acid Fuel Cell (PAFC)) or high temperature fuel cells (Molten Carbonate Fuel Cell (MCFC), Solid Oxide Fuel Cell(SOFC)). The choice of the fuel cell type depends on the gaseous fuel used and the heat utilisation. The investment costs of all biogas fuel cells are much higher than for engine driven BTTPs, amounting some 12 000 €/kW. As in the case of biogas micro-turbines, the research and development work in this area is targeting competitive costs for the future models.

7.50 Biogas upgrading (Biomethane production)

Biogas can be distributed through the existing natural gas networks and used for the same purposes as natural gas or it can be compressed and used as renewable vehicle fuel. Prior to injection into the natural gas grid or to utilisation as vehicle fuel, biogas must undergo an upgrading process, where all contaminants as well as carbon dioxide are removed and the content of methane increased from the usual 50-75% to more than 95%. The upgraded biogas is often named biomethane. Various technologies can be applied for removal of contaminants and for increasing the methane content of biogas.

Removal of carbon dioxide is done in order to reach the required Wobbe index of gas. When removing carbon dioxide from biogas, small amounts of methane CH4) are also removed. As methane has a 23-fold stronger greenhouse gas effect than CO_2, (i.e. a molecule of methane is 23 times more effective than a molecule of CO_2 in trapping the radiated heat from earth) it is important to keep methane losses low, for both economic and environmental reasons. Two common methods of removing carbon dioxide from biogas are absorption (water scrubbing, organic solvent scrubbing) and adsorption (pressure swing adsorption, PSA). Less frequently used are membrane separation, cryogenic separation and process internal upgrading, which is a relatively new method, currently under development.

The total cost for cleaning and upgrading biogas consists of investment costs and of operation and maintenance costs. In the case of investment costs, an important factor is the size of the plant. The total investment costs increase with increased plant capacity but investment per unit of installed capacity is lower for larger plants, compared to small ones. In the case of operation costs, the most expensive part of the treatment is the removal of carbon dioxide.

8.0 FLEXIBILITY OF BIOGAS
In an energy system marked by intermittent renewable energy, offsetting changes in supply and demand through flexibility options is becoming

increasingly important. Among the renewable energy technologies available today and used to control the production of electricity are, besides geothermal and hydro, bio-energy installations in general and biogas plants in particular. Combined with other flexibility options such as power grids, storage or demand management, flexible power generation facilities such as biogas plants are the very condition of the proper functioning of the future electricity system.

The growing needs of electric system flexibility primarily the result of temporal and geographical gap between demand and supply, and their variations. Infrastructure based on a distribution network (gas or electricity networks) overcome geographical distances. As for the temporal distances, it should differentiate according to the time involved. Thus, the electrical system has fluctuated very short term between supply and demand, on the order of a few seconds to several minutes, which can be compensated by different types of control energy.

In general, the flexibility of biogas plants is an electricity production in line with demand in order to leverage fluctuations in short-term price stock electricity. The objective of these approaches is flexibility to concentrate the production of electricity where the benefit is potentially high. To do this, it is generally necessary to separate the production of fermentation gas power generation by a cogeneration plant. Several approaches to flexibility of biogas plants may be relevant in the field:

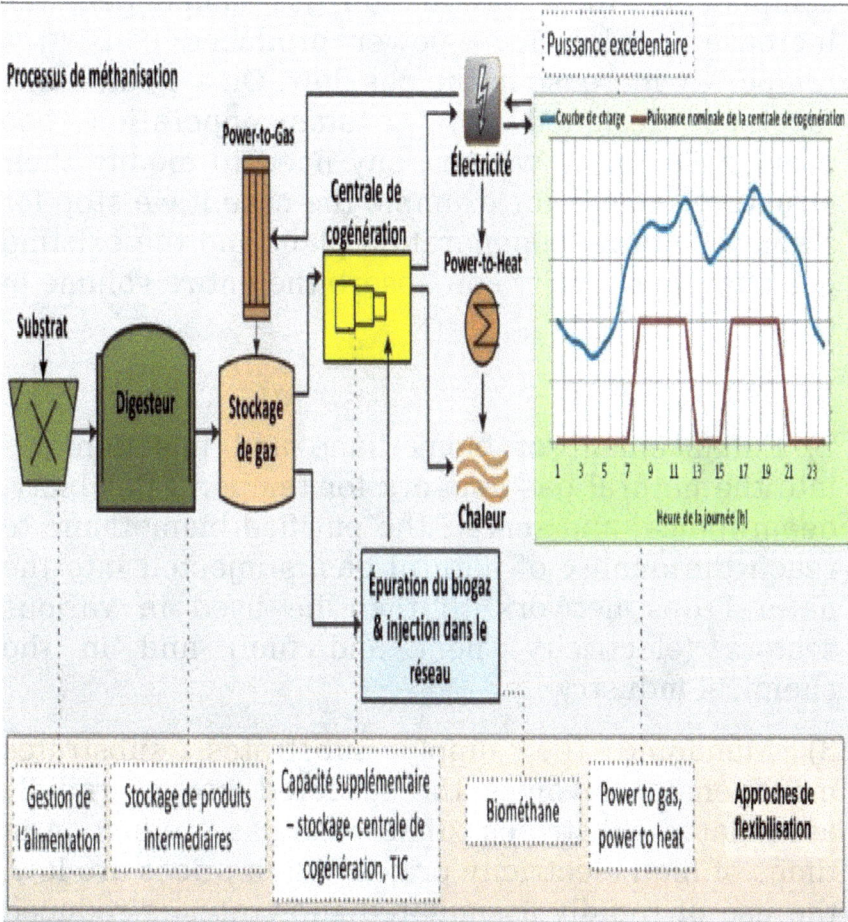

Figure 8:Flexibilisation of Biogas Plant

1)Technology used: capacity development in cogeneration and gas storage, as well as other components; for a production gas unchanged, the increase in electricity power produced causing a temporary increase in the gas flow. On a small scale, facilities designed for constant operation can provide flexibility without any need to modify their structure. This is for example the case if we stop for a short time the cogeneration plant and the existing gas storage capacity can absorb the entire volume of gas

2) Enhancement of biomethane and injection gas into the natural gas network for temporal flexibility, geographical and sector: the purified biomethane to reach the quality of natural gas is injected into the natural gas network to then be used in various sectors (electricity, heat and fuel) and in the chemical industry

3) Managing the supply substrates: substrates management involves the targeted use of rapidly assimilated substrates to increase gas production in times of high electricity prices. When prices are low, the use of rapidly assimilated substrates is reduced first. This approach can be combined with the storage of intermediate products of hydrolysis, used rapidly and in a targeted manner. In a broader sense, the reduction of substrates volumes also promotes medium and long-term flexibility. The total

volume of electricity produced, and therefore also the rated power, also will fall. The concepts of this type require less technical adaptations that those planning to maintain a constant total volume of electricity produced

4) Coupling sectors via the power-to-heat or power-to-gas: biogas, especially biogas plants offer opportunities for articulation with technologies to enhance electricity as heat (power-to -HEAT, P2H) or gas (power-to-gas, P2G). As part of the energy transition, the volume of surplus electricity will increase significantly in Germany from 2030/2035. Approaches based on the storage devices will be increasingly important to use so targeted surplus volumes and, to the extent possible, avoid power cuts. Depending on the scenario, the expected excess volumes in 2050 will reach about 154 TWh per year

COST ANALYSIS OF BIOGAS PLANTS

installed capacity (kW)	Investment $ USD	prices kWh ($ USD /kWh)
50	284371.99	0.18
100	551509.32	0.16
500	2085394.62	0.13
1000	2826485.27	0.0948

Conclusion and outlook

Biogas production is a natural process which is systematically done in biogas plants. A large variety of organic input materials are useable. The Fermentation process consists of four stages. Microorganisms are producing biogas in an anaerobic milieu at mesophile temperature. The produced raw biogas needs to be cleaned and upgraded to use it in various utilisation possibilities as electricity, heat and fuel. A large amount of biogas can be supplied by agriculture. Biogas production is regulated by many laws and regulations and economic success depends not only on societies support, but also on cost optimisation and highest use of the product. Biogas production is a chance for farmers to generate additional income. Efficiency and sustainability are the key elements for crop cultivation, biogas production and utilisation for the future.

The technology of treating toilet sewage applying biogas decontamination system is surely mature. It has contributed much to the sanitation and environmental protection of cities, and to the improvement of people's civilization and life quality. It is a way of less investment, high efficiency, obvious effectiveness, lasting usage time and low operating fee. It meets local conditions of middle or small sized cities, towns, sight spots and factory residents, as well as developing countries, which have no ability to build mechanical plant for integrative treatment of sewage. This technology is worth great disseminating and wide application.

CHAPTER TWO:

BRIQUETTE CHARCOAL

Briquette charcoal manufacture offers a solution to the problem of deforestation by providing an alternative to traditional wood charcoal. By using sawdust and other waste materials as raw materials, the production of briquettes reduces the demand for wood-based charcoal, thus lessening the pressure on forests. This can contribute to the preservation and regeneration of forests, which are crucial for biodiversity and ecosystem stability.

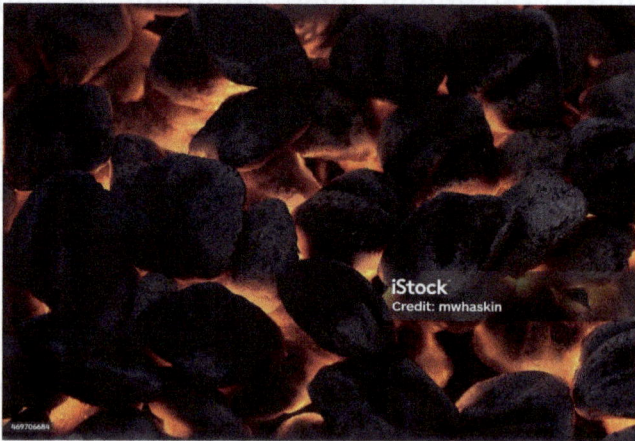

iStock
Credit: mwhaskin

The use of sawdust and other waste materials for briquette production helps in waste reduction and recycling efforts. Instead of disposing of these waste materials, they are repurposed into a valuable commodity. This promotes sustainable waste management practices and reduces the environmental impact of waste disposal.

Energy Security energy for cooking and heating, particularly in areas with electricity shortages and unreliable power supply. By providing an alternative energy source, briquette manufacture can contribute to improving energy security and ensuring access to affordable and reliable energy for households and businesses.

The establishment of briquette charcoal manufacturing businesses can stimulate local economies by creating jobs in manufacturing, distribution, and sales. This can provide employment opportunities and income generation for individuals and communities, contributing to economic development and poverty alleviation.

Briquettes have a lower carbon footprint compared to fossil fuels, such as coal. By using renewable materials and employing energy-efficient production processes, briquette charcoal manufacture can contribute to reducing greenhouse gas emissions and mitigating climate change. This aligns with global efforts to transition towards low-carbon and sustainable energy sources. he findings suggested that the use of agricultural waste briquette fuel for heating has great potential for carbon neutrality. The utilization of 100,000 tons of biomass briquette fuel by a heating enterprise resulted in a remarkable reduction of 335,679 tons of CO_2-eq, equivalent to 91,305 tons of carbon. This substitution also displaced 63,558 tons of coal, leading to a reduction of 5460 tons of SO_2 and 1012 tons of PM10. The sensitivity analysis identified that transportation distance, energy consumption, and pollutant removal technologies were the primary drivers influencing carbon reduction. Subsequently, some recommendations were proposed to enhance the carbon neutrality of biomass briquette fuel heating systems. These findings have significant implications for achieving carbon neutrality.

Overall, the application of briquette charcoal manufacture addresses environmental, economic, and social challenges, offering potential benefits in terms of sustainable resource management, waste reduction, energy security, economic development, and climate change mitigation. It represents an innovative and entrepreneurial approach to addressing pressing issues and promoting a transition towards a more sustainable and eco-friendly energy sector.

Properties of charcoal fines

Charcoal fines have a much lower purity than lump charcoal. The fines contain, in addition to charcoal, fragments, mineral sand and clay picked up from the earth and the surface of the fuelwood and its bark. The fine powdered charcoal produced from bark, twigs and leaves has a higher ash content than normal wood charcoal. Most of this undesired high ash material can be separated by screening the fines and rejecting undersize material passing, say, a 2 to 4 mm screen. This fine material may still contain more than 50% charcoal depending on the level of contamination but, nevertheless, it is difficult to find uses for it. Material retained on the screen will be mostly fragments of good charcoal and, after hammer-milling is suitable for briquetting. Fines cannot be burned by the usual simple charcoal burning methods and hence are more or less unsaleable. But if fines could be fully used, overall charcoal production would rise by 10 to 20%. Briquetting - turning fines into lumps of charcoal - seems an obvious answer. Unfortunately, experience has shown up to now that, though it is technically possible to briquette charcoal fines, the economics are not usually favourable, except where the price of lump charcoal is very high and the fines are available at a very low or zero cost.

The techniques of briquetting

Briquetting requires a binder to be mixed with the charcoal fines, a press to form the mixture into a cake or briquette which is then passed through a drying oven to cure or set it by drying out the water so that the briquette is strong enough to be used in the same burning apparatus as normal lump charcoal. Charcoal is a material totally lacking plasticity and hence needs addition of a sticking or agglomerating material to enable a briquette to be formed. The binder should preferably be combustible, though a non-combustible binder effective at low concentrations can be suitable. Starch is preferred as a binder though it is usually expensive. Highly plastic clays are suitable providing not more than about 15% is used. Tar and pitch from coal distillation or from charcoal retorts have been used for special purpose briquettes but they must be carbonised again before use to form a properly bonded briquette. They are of good quality but costly to produce.

The press for briquetting must be well designed, strongly built and capable of agglomerating the mixture of charcoal and binder sufficiently for it to be handled through the curing or drying process. The output of briquettes must justify the capital and running costs of the machine. Briquetting machines for charcoal are usually costly precision machines capable of a high output. Brick making presses have been used but there do not appear to be any commercially effective, really low cost machines for this purpose. Charcoal is quite abrasive so that equipment for screening fines, grinding, mixing them with binder, Briquetting and so on must be abrasive-resistant and well designed.

The binders which have been tried are many but, as stated, the most common effective binder is starch. About 4-8% of starch made into paste with hot water is adequate. First, the fines are dried and screened. Undersized fines are rejected and oversized hammermilled. This powder is blended with the starch paste and fed to the briquetting press. The briquettes are dried in a continuous oven at about 80°C. The starch sets through loss of water, binding the charcoal into a briquette which can be handled and burned like ordinary lump charcoal in domestic stoves and grates. Generally briquettes are not suitable for use as industrial charcoal in blast furnaces and foundry cupolas, since the bond disintegrates on slight heating. For this briquettes bonded with tar or pitch and subsequently carbonised in charcoal furnaces to produce a metallurgical charcoal briquette of adequate crushing strength are needed. The cost is too high for the process to find industrial application in most countries.

It is possible to add material to aid combustion of briquettes such as waxes, sodium nitrate, and so on, during manufacture to give a more acceptable product. Also clay as a binder, silica, and so on, can be mixed with the fines to reduce the cost of the briquette. This, of course, lowers the calorific value and is merely a form of adulteration for which the user pays, though claims may be made that burning is improved. But well made briquettes are an acceptable, convenient product. The virtual absence of fines and dust and their uniformity are attractive for barbecue purposes. Generally they sell at around the same cost per kg as lump charcoal in high price markets and have more or less the same calorific value as commercial charcoal of 10-15% moisture content.

Successful briquette operations are found mostly in developed countries. An example is the industry based on carbonization of sawdust and bark in the southern U.S.A. using rotary multiple hearth furnaces which produce perhaps 25 to 50 tons of fine charcoal per day. When briquetted, this charcoal, intended for barbecues, can be sold in retail outlets. The furnace gases are burned to produce steam of electric power, thus transforming the waste sawdust and bark into two useful products, electric power and charcoal briquettes. Air pollution and waste disposal problems are minimised at the same time.

Economics of briquetting

The cost of briquetting mainly depends on three factors. The cost of the fine charcoal delivered at the plant ready for processing, the cost of the binder and the incidence of capital costs. Fines which normally have little value, are usually reckoned to have zero cost to justify the briquette plant investment. However, this is not true because to supply the fines to the plant from sources, even close by, costs money. If the fines are not all derived from captive operations of the briquetting organization, it will be found that the price of purchased fines moves steadily upward as soon as the briquettes appear on the market. The binder of preference is starch which is a food material and costs about ten or more times the cost of raw lump charcoal at the side of the kiln. Hence, as a 4-8% addition to charcoal fines is needed to make the briquettes, it is a very significant cost item. Successful briquetting operations such as those operating in the U.S.A. and other developed countries depend on a favourable conjunction of factors which are usually absent in developing countries. They are:

- An established high priced household market for barbecue fuel.

- Ability to produce fine charcoal for briquettes at very low cost, close to major markets, and in steady volume through the year.

- A high volume of sales adequate to absorb the potential production of the plant.

- Adequate capital for good equipment and skilled labour for operations and maintenance.

- A proper marketing, packaging and distribution system to enable the product to achieve adequate market penetration at a rewarding price.

Generally speaking, and this is supported by the lack of successful briquetting operations in the developing world, it is better to concentrate attention on producing charcoal efficiently from fuelwood, striving for maximum conversion yield and minimum production of fines by careful handling of the product. Furthermore, such production using simple brick kilns requires a low level of imported components, whereas briquetting machinery is normally a costly imported item. Unless a briquette plant can be kept operating over the year at near full production, the capital charges become a drain on profitability.

Briquetting as a cottage industry

There is no doubt that unused charcoal fines are a waste of resources and alert management will always be seeking an economic outlet for them.

Unfortunately, there is no simple, really satisfactory means of briquetting them on a small scale industry level. It is possible by primitive means to press charcoal fines mixed with starch paste or clay in a mould and dry them, each cakes of charcoal are made in a number of countries but success depends on providing charcoal fines at a very low price to households. Normally this is not possible since fine charcoal in quantities is mainly to be found near the production centres and not in the cities where unpaid household labour is available to produce the product. But despite the difficulty, opportunities of this type should be closely studied in the interests of overall national fuel economy.

Using fine charcoal without briquetting

Charcoal fines when available in large quantities do have industrial uses. Unfortunately, the customary lack of a developed industrial infrastructure where charcoal is usually made in the developing world precludes using charcoal fines this way. The main industrial uses of fine charcoal are as fuel in metallurgical and calcinning operations. For example, in charcoal iron making fine charcoal can be injected at the base of the blast furnace with the air blast. About 5% of the total charcoal can be injected this way. The charcoal iron works in Wundowie, Australia, was able to use up all its fine charcoal this way. Fine charcoal is excellent for producing sinter, partially reduced iron ore, to provide a high grade feed to the blast furnace. This is one of the best ways to use charcoal fines as the amount which can be used is not limited to a percentage of the total as is the case of injection into the base of the blast furnace. (1, 22). Sintering with fine charcoal is used in Argentina and Brazil. Pulverised fine and lump charcoal can be burned in rotary furnaces producing cement clinker and calcium bauxite. Such cement plants operating in Kenya and Guyana are experimenting with pulverised charcoal for bauxite calcination.

Despite these possibilities, the fact remains that, for the typical charcoal producer, it is better to reduce fines production to the minimum by good charcoal making techniques, rather than invest money in a marginally economic production of wood from plantations or natural forests and to use this wood to expand profitable production of charcoal.

CHAPTER THREE WASTE HEAT RECOVERY

1.1 Definition

Waste heat is energy that is rejected to the environment. WHR can be defined as the process of capturing some portion of the heat that normally would be wasted, and delivering it to a device or process where it can be used as an effective, economical and environmentally friendly way to save energy. Large investments are presently incurred to exhaust waste heat to the atmosphere in the form of cooling towers, fin-fan coolers and very tall stacks for the disposal of flue gases. WHR has the potential to minimize these costs, and to reduce environmental impact along with several other benefits.

1.2 Sources of waste heat
Sources from which waste heat can be recovered, are classified according to the temperature ranges:

I. WH sources for high temperature (> 650°C) as Nickel refining furnace, steel electric arc furnace, hydrogen plants, glass melting furnace coke oven, copper refining furnace.

II. WH sources for medium temperature (230°C-650°C) like steam boiler exhaust, gas turbine exhaust, reciprocating engine exhaust, heat treating furnace, drying and baking ovens, cement kiln.

III. WH sources for low temperature (<230°C): for instance, hot processed liquids/solids; drying, baking and curing ovens, cooling water from furnace doors, annealing furnaces, air compressors, internal combustion engines, air conditioning and refrigeration condensers, exhaust gases exiting recovery devices in gasifier boilers, process steam condensate, ethylene furnaces, etc.

1.3 Potential of Waste Heat Recovery
The sources of waste heat as mentioned above can be found in industrial, commercial and domestic applications. the cement industry alone has a potential between 1615 and 2930 MW_e. The figure 1-1 below shows the waste heat potential and installed

capacity cement production sector of selected countries including South Africa, Egypt and Nigeria in Africa.

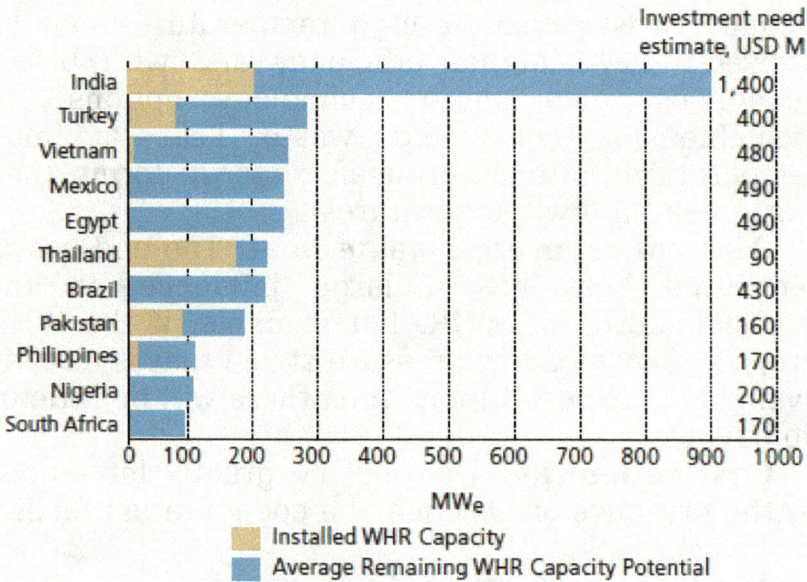

Figure 1-9: WH Potential of Selected Countries (ESI Africa 2013)

In the cement industry, in spite of the fact that many countries have Waste Heat Potential, most of them do not invest in waste heat recovery. This is the trend in several other industrial sectors.

1.4 Factors influencing Efficiency and Effectiveness of WHR systems

The efficiency of an optimum WHR system rely on the following factors:

I. **Quantity and temperature of waste heat:** The quantity of waste heat should be large enough to make WHR economical. Costs of WHR systems are lower with increased availability of waste heat. Usually, waste heat at high temperatures can be utilized with a higher efficiency and with better economics. Also, more technology options are available for converting waste heat at high temperatures into other useful energy forms than waste heat at low temperatures

II. **Uses of recovered waste heat:** The end use of recovered heat has a large influence on the implementation of WHR. For example, if the WHR project generates low-pressure steam that is already available in excess supply, then there will be little or no payout.

III. **Cost of energy:** This will be greatly influenced by the presence or absence of a cogeneration facility in the company.

IV. **Availability of space:** In operating plants, space availability can be the biggest constraint. It is beneficial to place WHR equipment close to the heat sink to minimize piping and operating costs

V. **Minimum allowable temperature of waste heat fluid:** For the case of flue gas heat recovery using carbon-steel equipment and ducting, the flue gas temperature should not be lower than the flue gas acid dew point.

VI. **Minimum and maximum temperature of the process fluid:** Low-temperature steam generation will result in more WHR compared to high-temperature steam generation

VII. **Chemical compositions of waste heat process fluids:** These will dictate the materials of construction for the WHR system, and consequently affect the costs

VIII. **Facility's heat-to-power ratio:** If the heat-to-power ratio in the facility is higher than that for the cogeneration plant, the excess steam demand is usually met by utility boilers. Any saving in steam demand (by better heat recovery) saves fuel in the utility boilers and leaves the operation of the cogeneration plant unchanged. However, if the cogeneration plant meets the entire site's heat load, the value of savings from better heat recovery can be considerably reduced. Saving a ton of steam not only saves the fuel required to raise it, but also eliminates the associated power output that is produced at 80–90% marginal efficiency

The factors started above determine the WHR and storage technologies to be used. The next sections discuss the WH recovery and storage technologies;

1.1   Waste Heat Recovery Technologies

Waste heat recovery technologies are divided into according to operation temperature ranges as;

1.1.1 Heat Exchangers

2.1.1.1 Medium to High Temperature WHR Technologies

According to U.S Department of Energy (2014) Medium temperature applications operate between 232 °C and 650 °C while the high temperature applications operate above 650 °C. The medium to high temperature WHR technologies are;

I. Regenerator

Regenerators are divided into;

a) Furnace Regenerator

Regenerative furnaces consist of two brick "checkerwork" chambers through which hot and cold air flow alternately. As combustion exhausts pass through one chamber, the bricks absorb heat from the combustion gas and increase in temperature. The flow of air is then adjusted so that the incoming combustion air passes through the hot checkerwork, which transfers heat to the combustion air entering the furnace as shown in the figure 2-1 below. Regenerator systems are especially suited for high temperature applications with dirty exhausts.

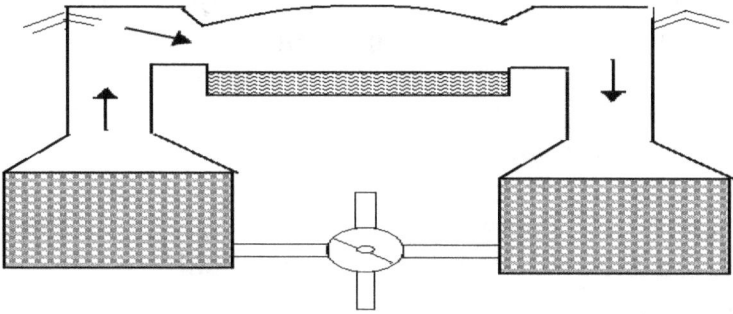

Figure 2-10: Regenerative Furnace (Turner et Doty 2006)

One major disadvantage is the large size and capital costs, which are significantly greater than costs of recuperators

b) Rotary Regenerator/Heat Wheel

Rotary regenerators operate similar to fixed regenerators in that heat transfer is facilitated by storing heat in a porous media, and by alternating the flow of hot and cold gases through the regenerator. Rotary regenerators, sometimes referred to as air preheaters and heat wheels, use a rotating porous disc placed across two parallel ducts, one containing the hot waste gas, the other containing cold gas. The disc, composed of a high heat capacity material, rotates between the two ducts and transfers heat from the hot gas duct to the cold gas duct.

One advantage of the heat wheel is that it can be designed to recover moisture as well as heat from clean gas streams. When designed with hygroscopic materials, moisture can be transferred from one duct to the other. This makes heat wheels particularly useful in air conditioning applications, where incoming hot humid air transfers heat and moisture to cold outgoing air. Besides its main application in space heating and air conditioning systems, heat wheels are also used to a limited extent in medium temperature applications

II. Recuperator

Recuperators recover exhaust gas waste heat in medium to high temperature applications such as soaking or annealing ovens, melting furnaces, afterburners, gas incinerators, radiant tube burners, and reheat furnaces. Recuperators can be based on radiation, convection, or combinations.

A simple radiation recuperator consists of two concentric lengths of ductwork. Hot waste gases pass through the inner duct and heat transfer is primarily radiated to the wall and to the cold incoming air in the outer shell. The preheated shell air then travels to the furnace burners. The convective or tube type recuperator (heat exchanger) passes the hot gases through relatively small diameter tubes contained in a larger shell. The incoming combustion air enters the shell and is baffled around the tubes, picking up heat from the waste gas. Another alternative is the combined radiation/convection recuperator. The system includes a radiation section followed by a convection section in order to maximize heat transfer effectiveness.

Recuperators are constructed out of either metallic or ceramic materials. Metallic recuperators are used in applications with temperatures below 1,093ºC, while heat recovery at higher temperatures is better suited to ceramic tube recuperators. These can operate with hot side temperatures as high as 1,538ºC and cold side temperatures of about 982ºC (Turner et Doty 2006). The figure 2-2 below shows the recuperator.

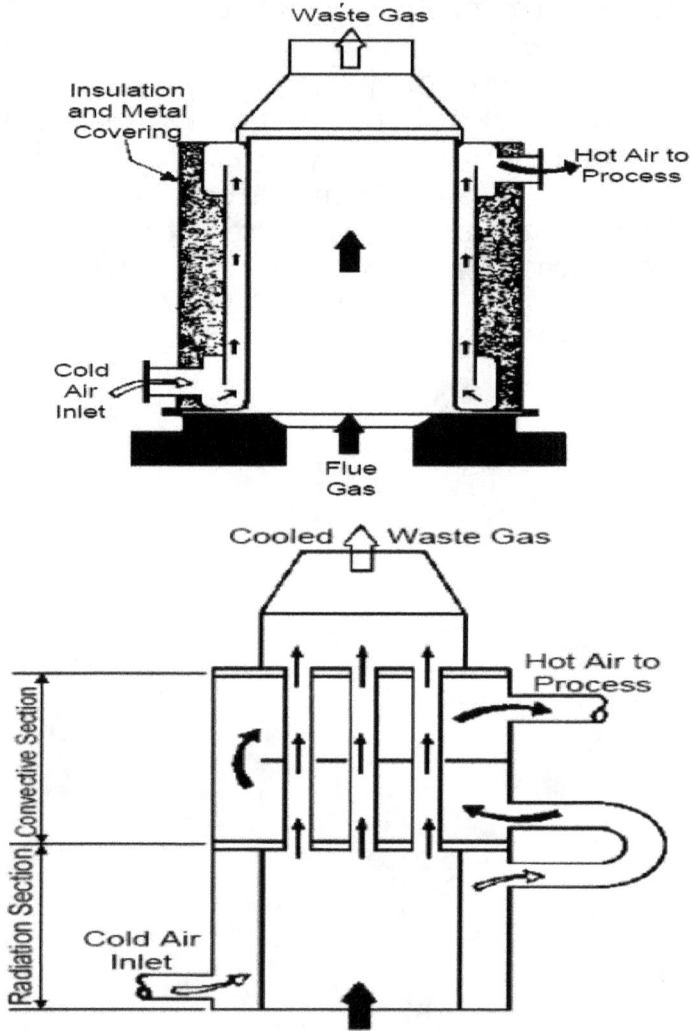

Figure 2-11: Radiation and convection recuperators (Turner et Doty 2006)

III.   Passive Air Preheaters

Passive air preheaters are gas to gas heat recovery devices for low to medium temperature applications where cross contamination between gas streams must be prevented. Applications include ovens, steam boilers, gas turbine exhaust, secondary recovery from furnaces, and recovery from conditioned air. The figure 2-3 below shows the passive air heater.

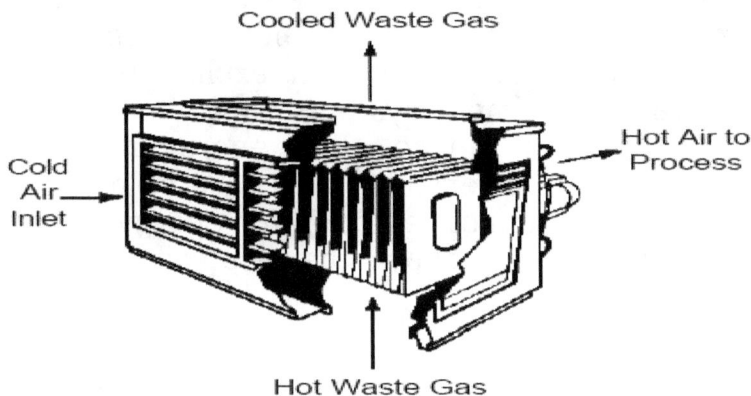

Figure 2-12: Passive air heater(Thekdi & Inc., 2015)

The heat pipe heat exchanger consists of several pipes with sealed ends. Each pipe contains a capillary wick structure that facilitates movement of the working fluid between the hot and cold ends of the pipe.

IV. Regenerative/Recuperative Burners

Burners that incorporate regenerative or recuperative systems are commercially available. Simpler and more compact in design and construction than a standalone regenerative furnaces or recuperators. These systems provide increased energy efficiency compared to burners operating with ambient air. A self-recuperative burner incorporates heat exchange surfaces as part of the burner body design in order to capture energy from the exiting flue gas, which passes back through the body. Self-regenerative burners pass exhaust gases through the burner body into a refractory media case and operate in pairs similar in manner to a regenerative furnace. Typically, recuperative burner systems have less heat exchange area and regenerative burner systems lower mass than standalone units. Hence, their energy recovery is lower but their lower costs and ease of retrofitting make them an attractive option for energy recovery. The figure 2-4 below shows the recuperative burner.

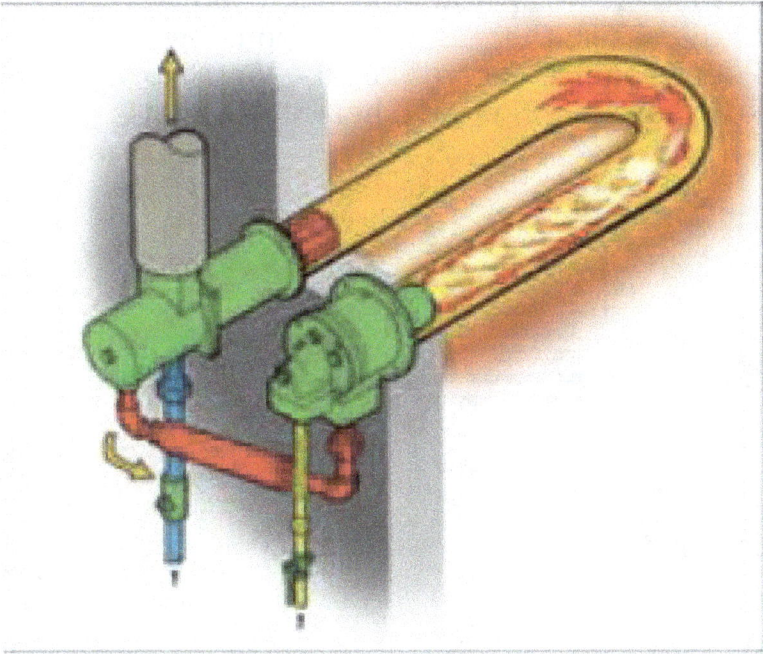

Figure 2.4: Recuperative burner (Thekdi & Inc., 2015)

V. Finned Tube Heat Exchangers/Economizers

Finned tube heat exchangers are used to recover heat from low to medium temperature exhaust gases for heating liquids. Applications include boiler feed-water preheating, hot process liquids, hot water for space heating, or domestic hot water. The finned tube consists of a round tube with attached fins that maximize surface area and heat transfer rates. In case of boiler system, economizer can be provided to utilize the flue gas heat for pre-heating the boiler feed water. On the other hand, in an air pre-heater, the waste heat is used to heat combustion air. In both the cases, there is a corresponding reduction in the fuel requirement of the boiler. The figure 2-5 below shows the fine tube heat exchanger.

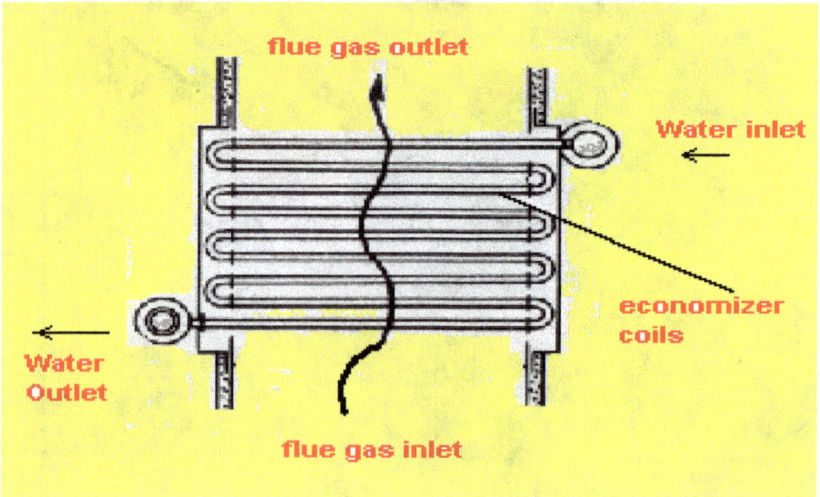

flue gas outlet

Water inlet

economizer coils

Water Outlet

flue gas inlet

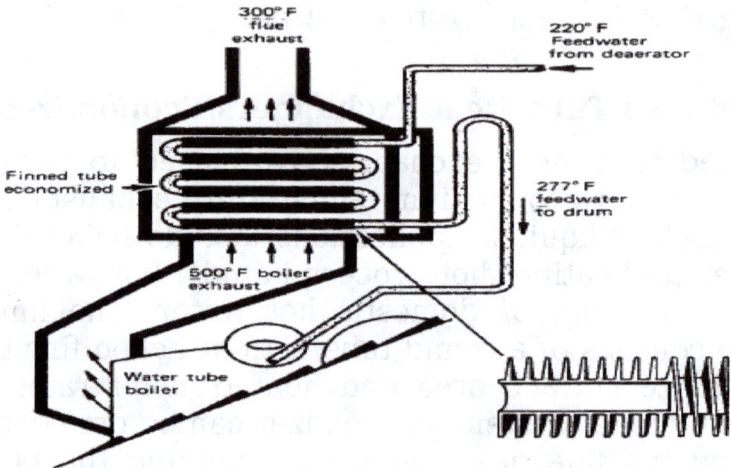

300° F flue exhaust

220° F Feedwater from deaerator

Finned tube economized

277° F feedwater to drum

500° F boiler exhaust

Water tube boiler

Figure 13.5: Finned Tube Exchanger/Boiler Economizer (Turner & Steve, 2007)

VI. Waste Heat Boilers

Waste heat boilers are ordinarily water tube boilers in which the hot exhaust gases from gas turbines, incinerators, etc., pass over a number of parallel tubes containing water. The water is vaporized in the tubes and collected in a steam drum from which it is drawn off for use as heating or processing steam. The steam can be used for process heating or for power generation. Generation of superheated steam will require addition of an external super heater to the system. The figure 2-6 below shows a waste heat boiler.

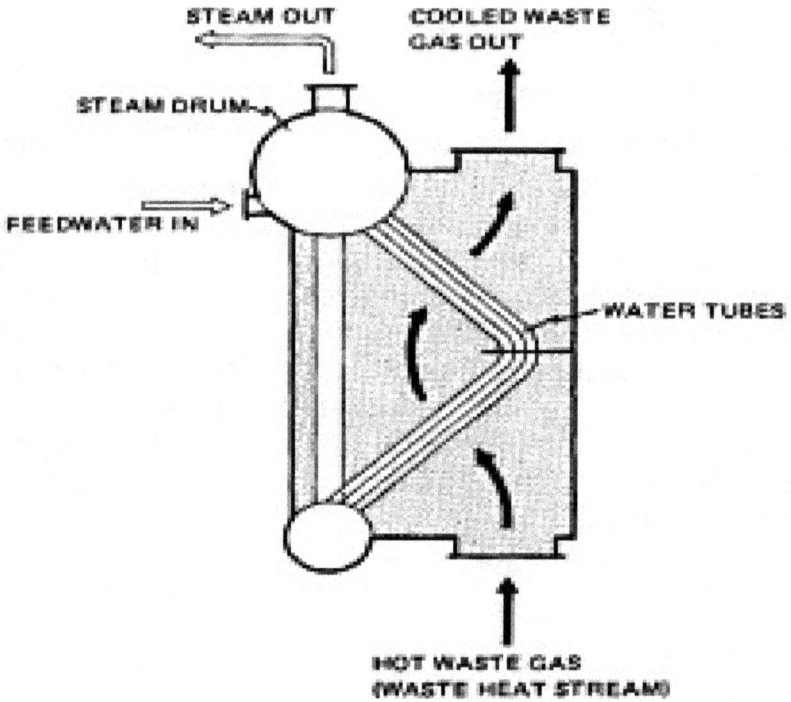

STEAM OUT

COOLED WASTE
GAS OUT

STEAM DRUM

FEEDWATER IN

WATER TUBES

HOT WASTE GAS
(WASTE HEAT STREAM)

Figure 2.6: Waste Heat Boiler (Turner & Steve, 2007)

VII.   Load Preheating

Load preheating refers to any efforts to use waste heat leaving a system to preheat the load entering the system. The most common example is boiler feed water preheating, where an economizer transfers heat from hot combustion exhaust gases to the water entering the boiler. Other applications utilize direct heat transfer between combustion exhaust gases and solid materials entering the furnace. For example, in the aluminum metal casting industry, stack melters can replace reverberatory furnaces to reduce energy consumption.

2.1.1.2 Low Temperature WHR Technologies

According to the U.S Department of Energy (2014), low temperature WHR recovery applications are those operating below 232 °C. Some of the low temperature WHR technologies are as mentioned below.

I. Low Temperature Heat Exchangers
a) Deep Economizers

Deep economizers are designed to cool exhaust gas to between 65ºC and 71ºC and to withstand the acidic condensate depositing on its surface.

b) Indirect Contact Condensation Recovery

Indirect contact condensation recovery unit cools gases to temperature between 38°Cand 43ºC. In this range, the water vapour in gases will condense almost completely. Indirect contact exchangers consist of shell & tube heat exchangers.

c) Shell and Tube Heat Exchanger:

The shell contains the tube bundle, and usually internal baffles, to direct the fluid in the shell over the tubes in multiple passes. The shell is inherently weaker than the tubes so that the higher-pressure fluid is circulated in the tubes while the lower pressure fluid flows through the shell. When a vapour contains the waste heat, it usually condenses, giving up its latent heat to the liquid being heated. In this application, the vapour is almost invariably contained within the shell.

d) Direct Contact Condensation Recovery

Direct contact condensation recovery involves direct mixing of the process stream and cooling fluid. Since these systems do not involve a separating wall across which heat must be transferred, they avoid some of the challenges of large heat transfer surfaces required for indirect contact units.

e) Transport Membrane Condenser

Transport Membrane Condensers (TMCs) are a developing technology for capturing water (along with water's latent heat) from the water vapour in gas exhaust streams. Water is extracted from the flue gas at temperatures above dew point by employing capillary condensation and recycled into the boiler feed water Transport Membrane Condenser

f) Heat Pumps (Upgrading Low Temperature Waste Heat)

Heat exchange technologies described above involve flow of energy "downhill" from a high temperature to a lower temperature end-use. This can place limitations on opportunities for heat recovery when the waste heat temperature is below the temperature needed for a given heating load. (For example, waste heat may be available in the form of hot water at 90ºF [32ºC], while hot water at 82ºC is needed elsewhere in the facility). In such cases, a heat pump may provide opportunities for "upgrading" heat to the desired end-use temperature. Heat pumps use external energy inputs to drive a cycle that absorbs energy from a low temperature source and rejects it at a higher temperature. Depending on the design, heat pumps can serve two functions: either upgrading waste heat to a higher temperature, or using waste heat as an energy input for driving an absorption cooling system. Heat pumps are most applicable to low temperature product streams found in process industries including chemicals, petroleum refining, pulp and paper, and food processing. The table 2-7 below compares the losses from a boiler and heat pump.

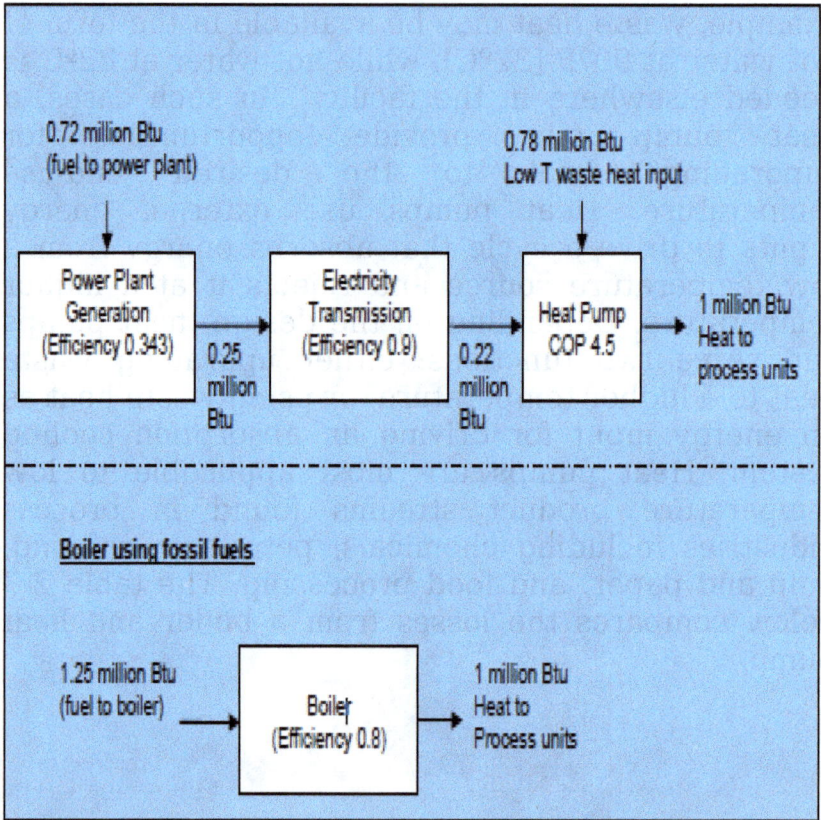

Figure 2-7: Energy losses from a boiler versus a heat pump (Hodges, 2009)

Upgrading heat can be economical in some cases depending on the temperature differential required and the relative costs of fuel and electricity. If a facility has a heat load at a slightly higher temperature than the waste heat source, the heat can sometimes be provided more efficiently by a heat pump than if it were obtained from burning additional fossil fuels. Figure 16 displays typical energy losses associated with a heat pump and a steam boiler. In this example, the boiler requires 1.25 million Btu fuel input to provide 1 million Btu of heat. Meanwhile, the heat pump requires an input of only 0.72 Million Btu for electricity generation in conjunction with the 0.78 Million Btu already available from the waste heat stream.

g) Absorption Chillers

Absorption heat pumps can also be used as chillers, which use thermal rather than mechanical energy for operation. Absorption chillers generally employ either LiBr or ammonia absorption in water. LiBr-water systems are limited to evaporation temperatures above freezing, because water is used as the refrigerant.

2.1.2 Power Generation Technologies using waste Heat

The technologies for power generation from waste heat can be divided into direct and indirect methods as below;

2.1.2.1 Indirect Power Generation

I. Steam Rankine Cycle

The most frequently used system for power generation from waste heat involves using the heat to generate steam, which then drives a steam turbine. The traditional steam Rankine cycle is the most efficient option for waste heat recovery from exhaust streams with temperatures between 340-370°C. At lower waste heat temperatures, steam cycles become less cost effective, since low pressure steam will require sources. Waste heat recovery can be applied to a variety of low to medium temperature heat streams. The figure 2.8 below shows schematic diagram of ORC.

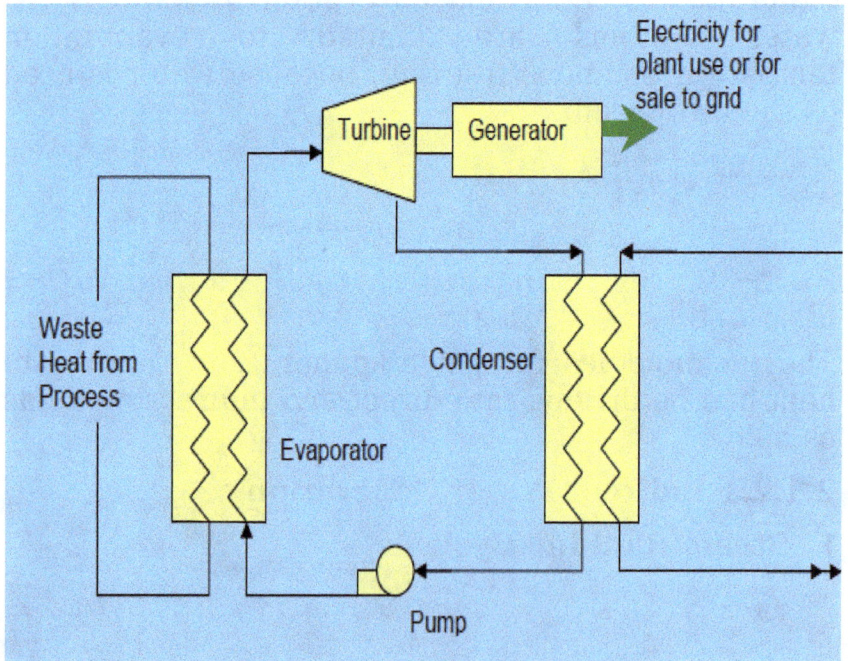

Figure 2.8: Organic Rankin Cycle (BCS, 2008)

II. Kalina Cycle

The Kalina cycle is a variation of the Rankine cycle, using a mixture of ammonia and water as the working fluid. A key difference between single fluid cycles and cycles that use binary fluids is the temperature profile during boiling and condensation. For single fluid cycles (e.g., steam or organic Rankine), the temperature remains constant during boiling. As heat is transferred to the working medium (e.g., water), the water temperature slowly increases to boiling temperature, at which point the temperature remains constant until all the water has evaporated. In contrast, a binary mixture of water and ammonia (each of which has a different boiling point) will increase its temperature during evaporation. This allows better thermal matching with the waste heat source and with the cooling medium in the condenser. Consequently, these systems achieve significantly greater energy efficiency. The figure 2.9 below shows schematic diagram of the Kalina cycle.

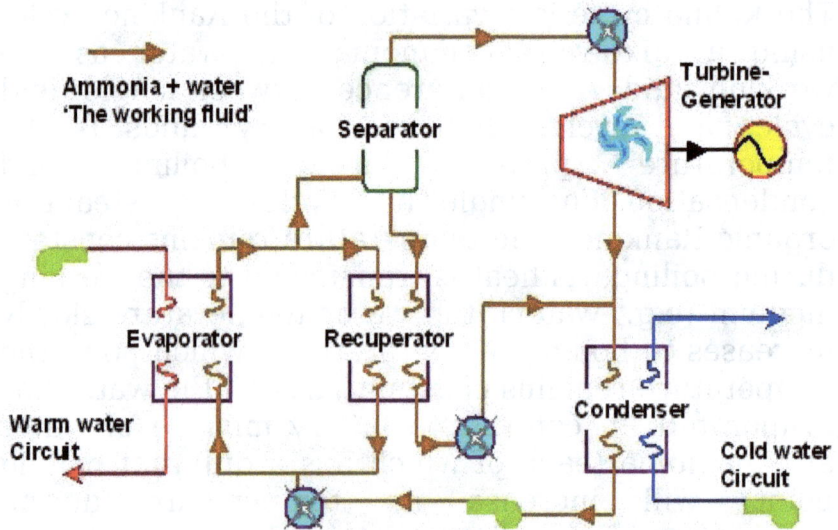

Figure 2.9: Kalina cycle (BCS, 2008)

2.1.2.2 Direct Electrical Conversion Devices

The direct power generation technologies are new and have only been tested at prototype level. Such direct technologies include;

I. Thermoelectric Generation

Thermoelectric (TE) materials are semiconductor solids that allow direct generation of electricity when subject to a temperature differential. These systems are based on a phenomenon known as the Seebeck effect: when two different semiconductor materials are subjected to a heat source and heat sink, a voltage is created between the two semiconductors. Conversely, TE materials can also be used for cooling or heating by applying electricity to dissimilar semiconductors. The figure 2.10 below shows the thermoelectric generator.

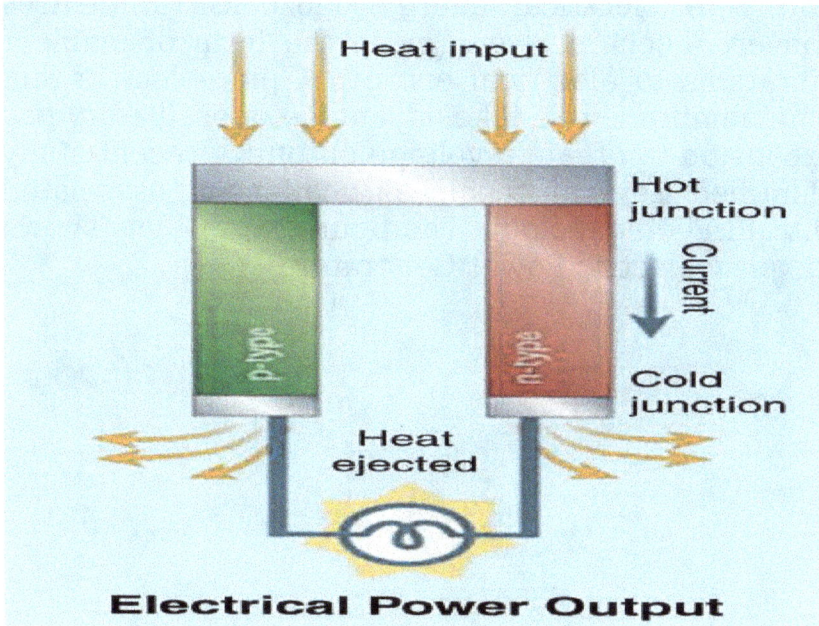

Figure 2.10: Thermoelectric generation unit (BCS, 2008)

Most TE generation systems in use have efficiencies of 2 to 5%; these have mainly been used to power instruments on spacecraft or in very remote locations. However, recent advances in nanotechnology have enabled advanced TE materials that might achieve conversion efficiencies 15% or greater. Two example opportunities are glass furnaces and molten metal furnaces.

II. Piezoelectric Power Generation

Piezoelectric Power Generation (PEPG) is an option for converting low temperature waste heat 100°C - 150°C to electrical energy. Piezoelectric devices convert mechanical energy in the form of ambient vibrations to electrical energy. A piezoelectric thin film membrane can take advantage of oscillatory gas expansion to create a voltage output. A recent study identified several technical challenges associated with PEPG technology. The figure 2-11 below shows the piezoelectric Power Generator.

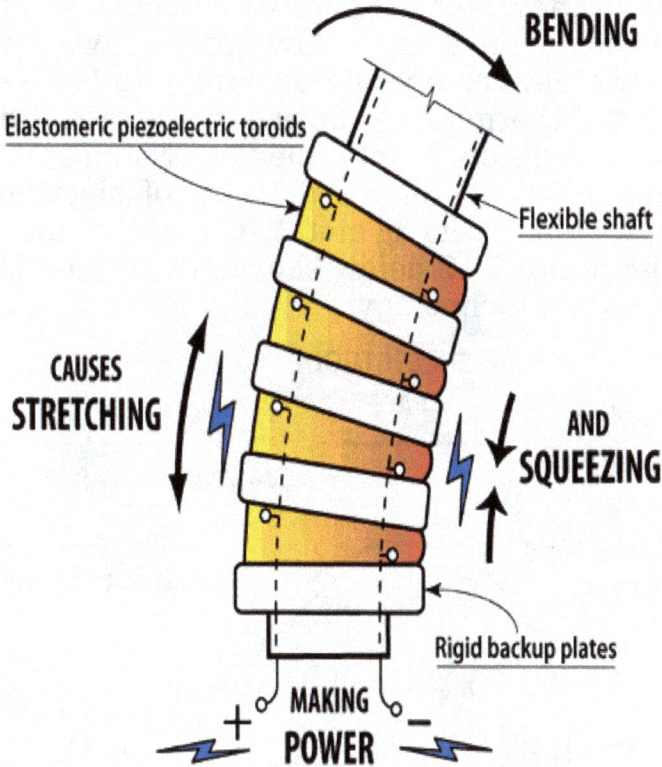

Figure 2.11: Piezoelectric power generation (Hodges, 2009)

The technology is characterised by low efficiency of 1 %, high levellised cost of $10,000/W, high internal impedance and complex oscillatory fluid dynamics.

III.   Thermionic Generation

Thermionic devices operate similar to thermoelectric devices; however, whereas thermoelectric devices operate according to the See beck effect, thermionic devices operate via thermionic emission. In these systems, a temperature difference drives the flow of electrons through a vacuum from a metal to a metal oxide surface. The figure 2.12 below shows the thermionic power generation technology.

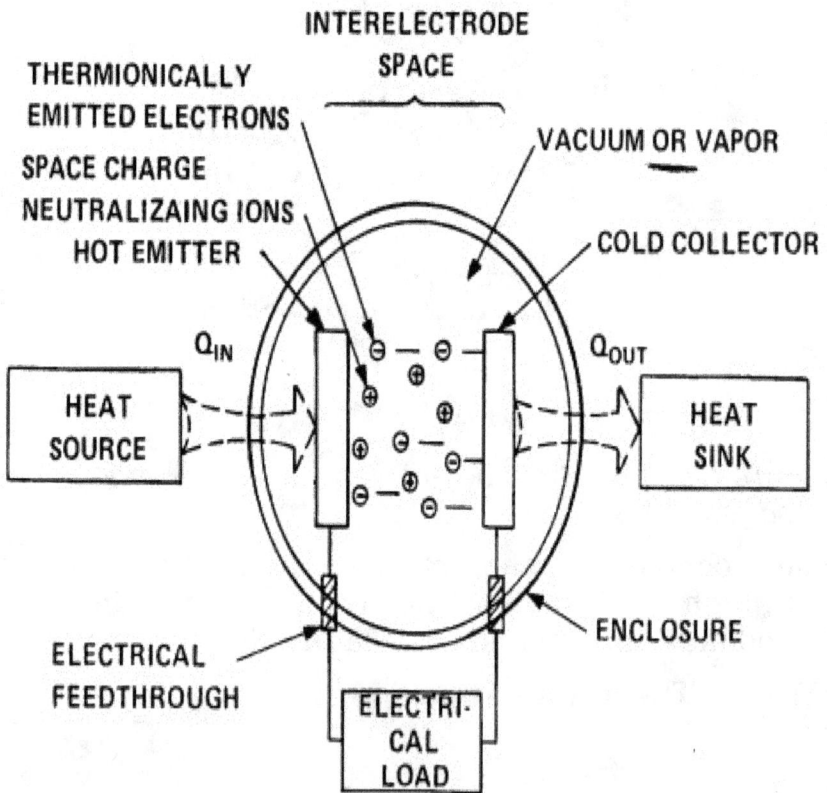

Figure 2.12: Thermionic generation (Instestellar Data Express, 2010)

One key disadvantage of these systems is that they are limited to applications with high temperatures above 1,000°C. However, some development has enabled their use at about 100-300°C.

IV.   Thermo-Photo Voltaic (TPV) Generator

TPV Generators can be used to convert radiant energy into electricity. These systems involve a heat source, an emitter, a radiation filter, and a PV cell (like those used in solar panels). As the emitter is heated, it emits electromagnetic radiation. The PV cell converts this radiation to electrical energy. The filter is used to pass radiation at wavelengths that match the PV cell, while reflecting remaining energy back to the emitter. These systems could potentially enable new methods for waste heat recovery. A small number of prototype systems have been built for small burner applications and in a helicopter gas turbine. The figure 2.9 below shows the TPV generator.

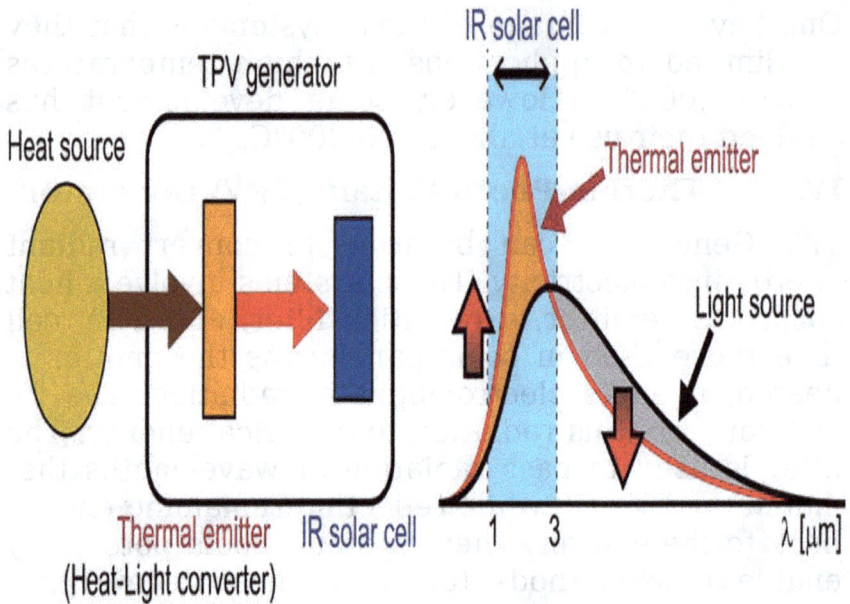

Figure 2.13: TPV Generator (Ueba, Yosuke; Takahara, Junichi, 2016)

II.2   Thermal Storage Technologies

Thermal energy (i.e. heat and cold) can be stored as sensible heat in heat storage media, as latent heat associated with phase change materials (PCMs) or as thermo-chemical energy associated with chemical reactions (i.e. thermo-chemical storage) at operation temperatures ranging from -40°C to above 400°C. Thermal Energy systems are shown in Table 2.2 and table 2-3 including capacity, power, efficiency, storage period and costs.

Table 2. 2: Parameters of Thermal Energy Storage Systems (IEA-ETSAP and IRENA 2013)

TES System	Capacity (kWh/t)	Power MW)	Efficiency (%)	Storage period (h, d, m)	Cost (€/kWh)
Sensible (hot water)	10-50	0.001-10	50-90	d/m	0.1-10
PCM	50-150	0.001-1	75-90	h/m	10-50
Chemical reactions	120-250	0.01-1	75-100	h/d	8-100

Technical performance	Typical current international values and ranges		
Energy Input/Output	Solar heat, waste heat, variable renewable energy sources (PV, wind), electricity/heat		
Technology Variants	Sensible Thermal Energy Storage, **STES**	Storage in Phase Change Materials, **PCM**	Thermo-chemical Energy Storage, **TCS**
Storage Capacity (kWh/t)	10 - 50	50 - 150	120 - 250
Thermal Power (MW)	0.001 - 10	0.001 - 1	0.01 - 1
Efficiency, %	50 - 90	75 - 90	75 - 100
Storage Period (h,d,w,m)	d - y	h - w	h - d
Cost (€/kWh)	0.1 - 10	10 - 50	8 - 100
Technical lifetime, yr	10-30+ (depending on storage cycles, temperature and operating conditions)		
Load (capacity) factor, %	80	80	55
Max. (plant) availability, %	95	95	95
Typical (capacity) size, MW	25	0.5	100
Installed capacity, GW, (GW_e)	9-10 (all types)	<<1	18 (estimate)
Environmental Impact	Negligible, with GHG emissions reduction, depending on the amount of primary fossil energy saved by using energy storage		
Costs (USD 2008)	**Typical current international values and ranges**		
Investment cost, $/kW	3400 - 4500	6000 - 15,000	1000 - 3000
O&M cost (fixed & variable), $/kW/a	120	250	20 - 60
Fuel cost, $/MWh	N/A	N/A	N/A
Economic lifetime, yr		20	
Total production cost, $/MWh	80 - 110	120 - 300	25 - 75
Market share, %	0.25	Negligible	N/A

Benefits of waste heat recovery can be broadly classified in two categories:

I. Direct Benefits:

Recovery of waste heat has a direct effect on the efficiency of the process. This is reflected by reduction in the utility consumption & costs, and process cost.

II. Indirect Benefits:

a) **Reduction in pollution:** A number of toxic combustible wastes such as carbon monoxide gas, sour gas, carbon black off gases, oil sludge, Acrylonitrile and other plastic chemicals etc, releasing to atmosphere when burnt in the incinerators serves dual purpose i.e. recovers heat and reduces the environmental pollution levels.

b) **Reduction in equipment sizes:** Waste heat recovery reduces the fuel consumption, which leads to reduction in the flue gas produced. This results in reduction in equipment sizes of all flue gas handling equipment such as fans, stacks, ducts, burners, etc.

c) **Reduction in auxiliary energy consumption:** Reduction in equipment sizes gives additional benefits in the form of reduction in auxiliary energy consumption like electricity for fans, pumps etc.

Disadvantages:

• **Capital cost:** The capital cost to implement a waste heat recovery system may outweigh the benefit gained in heat recovered. It is necessary to put a cost to the heat being offset.

•   **Quality of heat:** Often waste heat is of low quality (temperature). It can be difficult to efficiently utilize the quantity of low quality heat contained in a waste heat medium. Heat exchangers tend to be larger to recover significant quantities which increases capital cost.

•   **Maintenance of Equipment**: Additional equipment requires additional maintenance cost.

•   Units add addition size and mass to overall power unit. Especially a consideration on power units which are on vehicles.

.1 Traditional Domestic Waste Heat Recovery

In Africa traditional domestic WHR is done mostly for thermal use but not for electricity generation. Waste Heat Recovery is done in some communities during cooking and drying of agricultural products such as maize. The figure 4.1 below shows the traditional WHR practices in Africa.

Reignite © By Fernando M

109

Figure 4.1: Traditional WHR Practices in Africa
(Holcim 2013)

There is so far no research on how much energy is saved from such traditional domestic waste heat recovery processes.

1.2   Industrial WHR Projects

I. IPP project for waste heat recovery at South Africa platinum smelter

The US$12 million independent power producer (IPP) project was initiated by Anglo Platinum on 9 May 2013. The project aimed at recovering waste heat energy from platinum converting process at Waterval smelter complex in Rustenburg. In the past this process was undertaken using air-based fans. The new process uses a high pressure water system in which the extraction of waste heat is achieved by implementing an organic Rankine cycle technology.

The project harvests a total of 20 MW, uses 16.25 MW for internal operations and returns 3.75 MW_e into the grid. The total cost of energy saved is estimated to be worth US$1.5 million (ESI Africa 2013).The process achieves carbon emission savings of 19,000 tonnes of CO_2 a year, which based on 2013 carbon tax proposals in South Africa saves US$3 million (ESI Africa 2013).

i. **Sinima Cement Project – Angola**

Sinoma Cement plant in Angola produces 18 MW from Waste Heat Recovery. The method is a low temperature application that uses the Organic Rankine Cycle. I was commissioned in 2013.

2. Conclusion

Waste heat sources exit all around us in homes, commercial entities and industries. The Africans have done less in regards to harnessing waste heat. Traditionally Africans have been carrying out waste heat recovery. No research has been done to on the amount of energy saved in the waste heat recovery practices in traditional African homes. Waste heat can be recovered and used for heating or it can be used for producing electricity. Before setting up a waste heat recovery plant a situational analysis must be carried out to come up with the best. Since much of the WHR technologies are practiced in rest of the world except Africa. For African applications the systems should be redesigned to suit the African conditions. There must be more effort put in improving the traditional energy recovery practices at household level.

CHAPTER FOUR : HARNESSING SUN'S ENERGY

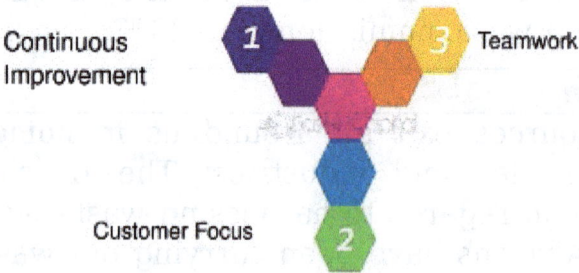

Kaizen's innovative approach to harnessing solar energy through quantum dot solar cells presents a game-changing solution to the energy crisis in Africa. By maximizing solar energy capture, boosting efficiency, and lowering costs, Kaizen addresses the critical issue of limited access to clean and affordable electricity in the continent. This not only benefits households by providing reliable energy sources but also empowers businesses to operate at full capacity, expand operations, and create new jobs. The potential for increased innovation in sectors like agriculture and manufacturing is significant, as reliable electricity is essential for growth and development.

Furthermore, Kaizen's emphasis on environmental sustainability by reducing reliance on fossil fuels not only tackles air pollution but also secures a cleaner future for Africa. The reduction in healthcare costs associated with pollution and the overall improvement in air quality will have long-lasting benefits for communities and governments. Additionally, combating load shedding through consistent electricity supply ensures that vital services like healthcare can operate without interruptions, ultimately improving the quality of life for all citizens.

The prospect of transitioning from fossil fuels to clean solar energy with Kaizen also holds promise for future generations in Africa. By investing in sustainable energy solutions now, we are paving the way for a more sustainable future for our children and grandchildren. This shift towards clean energy not only benefits the environment but also has the potential to drive economic growth, create jobs, and improve overall well-being for all Africans. In summary, Kaizen's transformative technology not only addresses the urgent need for clean and affordable electricity in Africa but also offers a pathway towards sustainable development, economic growth, and a cleaner future for generations to come. The opportunities and prospects for exploring this technology are vast and have the potential to reshape the energy landscape in Africa for the better.

Approaches for Harnessing Sun's Energy

Silicon Based Solar Cells

There are many initiatives solving our energy problems and most efficient and popular one is the silicon based solar cells. The lab based performance of silicon based solar cell has recently reached about 25%; however, market based efficiency is lower in the range of 15%–22.4%. In this year, the market based silicon solar panel produced by Suntech has an efficiency of 15.7%; however, solar panel installed by the Sun Power has a record efficiency of 22.4%.

Although silicon solar cells made by mono, multi crystalline, and amorphous thin films share about 85% of today's market, the major cost factors related with silicon based solar cell include requirements of high purity silicon, high preparation temperature, and large amount of materials in order to prepare a tiny cell. A report on cost profile of PV technologies disclosed that monocrystalline, multi crystalline, and amorphous silicon based solar panels cost $3.83, $3.43, and $3.00, respectively which are comparatively higher than other solar panels. However, in a recent interview, Stuart Wenham, chief technology officer of the Suntech Power, claimed that the recent prize of a cell module is reduced to US$1.5 W$-1$ from the previous prize of US$4 W$-1$. Despite many challenges with silicon wafer based solar cells, it is expected that silicon based photovoltaic technology will be dominated in the future market.

Dye Sensitized Solar Cells

Dye-sensitized solar cells (DSCs) invented by Michael Grätzel became a very popular alternative to silicon based solar cells because of their great potential to convert solar energy into electric energy at low cost. This cell can be made from cheap materials such as inorganic and organic dyes which do not need to be highly pure as is required for silicon wafer. The working principle of the solar cell is presented in Figure 3A. Here we can see inorganic dye is anchored to a wide bandgap mesoscopic semiconductor. The popular dyes used for DSC are ruthenium bipyridine and zinc porphyrin complexes. For a mesoscopic semiconductor, TiO2 (anatase) is widely used in the solar cells; however, other alternative metal oxides such as ZnO, SnO2 and Nb2O5 can be used. After excitation of dye by light, the dye releases its electron from the HOMO (highest occupied molecular orbital) to the LUMO (lowest unoccupied molecular orbital). This photoelectron then swiftly transfers from the LUMO of the dye to the conduction band of the semiconductor TiO2. The semiconductor carries the electron to the photoanode which passes the electron to the platinized counter electrode. Regeneration of the oxidized dye takes place by a redox couple such as iodide/triodide which reduces the dye by providing a continuous supply of electrons. Over many years, the overall conversion efficiency of most solar cells was unchanged from 11.18%. Only recently, Grätzel group was able to exceed the power conversion efficiency 12.3%.

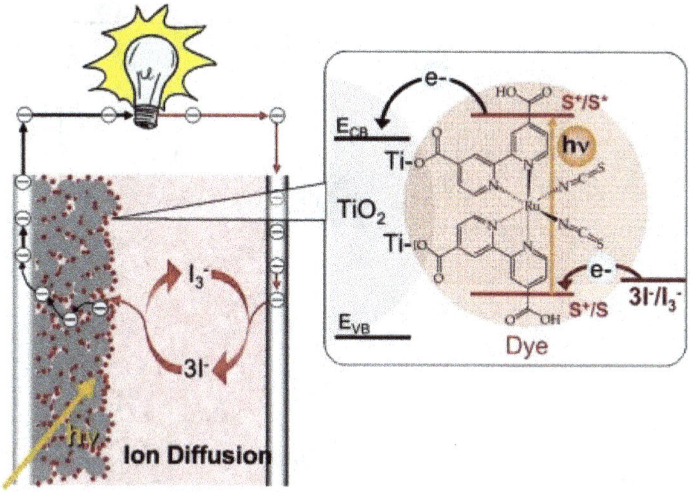

e-
E_{CB}
Ti-
TiO_2
Ti-
E_{VB}
S*/S*
hv
e-
3I⁻/I₃⁻
S⁺/S
Dye
I_3^-
$3I^-$
hv
Ion Diffusion

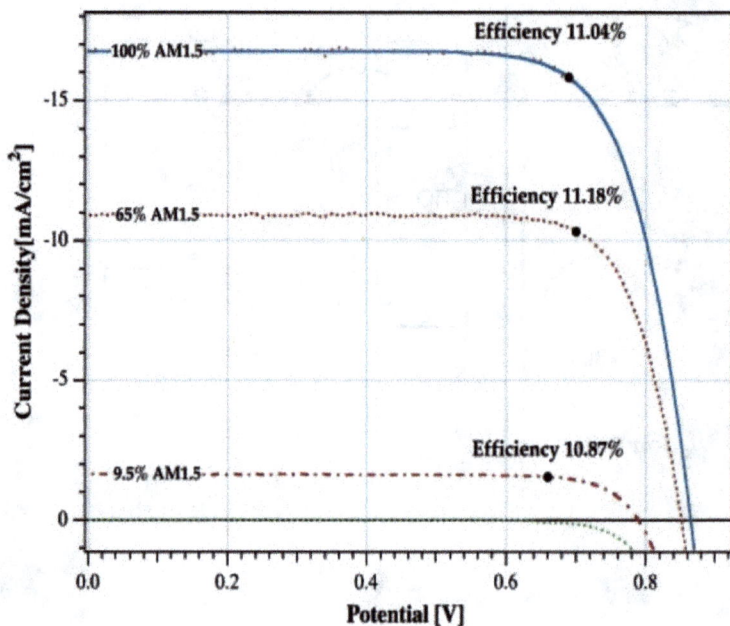

The dye sensitized solar cell; (B) PV curves show the power conversion efficiency of dye sensitized solar cell in different light intensities.

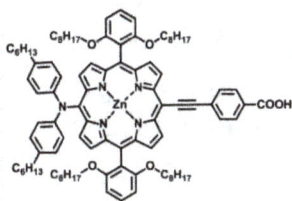

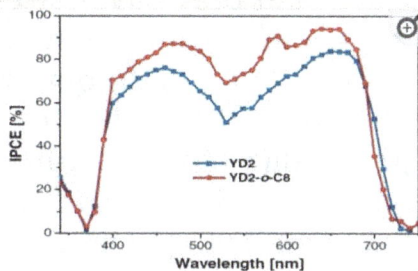

(A)　　　　　　　　　　　　(B)

Organic Solar Cells

The seminal work of Heeger, Shirakawa and MacDiarmid (winners of 2000 Nobel Prize in Chemistry) opened a new window to use organic conducting polymer for wide range of semiconductor devices such as light emitting diodes, solar cells, and thin film transistors. The motivation of developing organic materials for solar cell is to reduce the cost related to raw materials and manufacturing. Solarmer and Konarka Power Plastic, two US based companies, produce flexible polymer solar cells for many applications including portable electronics, smart fabrics, and integrated solar cells. The lab based power conversion efficiency of the polymer based single solar cells is reached to 8.6% reported by several groups.

Two well-known challenges associated with the donor-acceptor based polymer solar cell are that these polymers cannot cover the sun's broad spectrum due to their comparatively high bandgap

(1.6–2.0 eV) and they have lower carrier mobility. In order to exploit light from sun's full spectrum, recently Dou et al. (2019) developed a pyrrole (DPP) and dithiopene (BDT) based conjugated polymer poly{2,6'-4,8-di(5-ethylhexylthienyl)benzo[1,2-b;3,4-b]dithiophene-alt-5-dibutyloctyl-3,6-bis(5-bromothiophen-2-yl)pyrrolo[3,4-c]pyrrole-1,4-dione} (PBDTT-DPP) having a bandgap of 1.44 eV. This conjugated polymer has relatively higher carrier mobility. The tandem cell was constructed using Poly(3-hexylthiophene) (P3HT) and indene-C60 bis-adduct (IC60BA) as front-cell materials, and PBDTT-DPP together with the acceptor phenyl-c71-butyric acid methyl ester (PC71BM) as back-cell materials as shown in Figure 5 (bottom). Very recently, the solution phase tandem polymer based solar cell is achieved a record highest efficiency of 10.6% which is certified by NREL. The life time of the polymer based solar cell (PSC) is comparatively low to 3–7 years which is one of the major challenges of PSC facing in market.

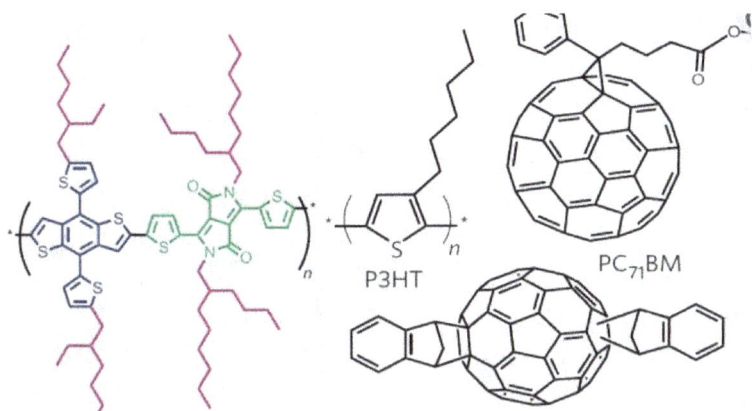

P3HT   PC₇₁BM

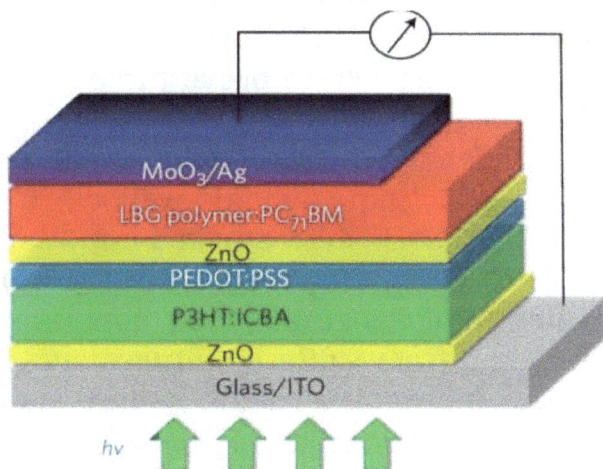

Cadmium Quantum Dots Based Solar Cells

Cadmium sulfide (CdS) and cadmium selenide (CdSe) are the two most studied quantum dots related to solar cell application. The reason for their widespread use is that they can be prepared easily and can be processed in solution. The first air stable bilayer cell of nanocrystalline CdTe/CdS exhibited a remarkable performance with an overall power conversion efficiency of 2.9% [42]. One earlier ultrafast absorption and emission study by Robel et al. [43] with CdSe quantum dot employing bifunctional surface modifier HS-R-COOH proved that CdSe can inject electron from its excited state to the mesoscopic TiO2. Although the cell exhibited the photon-to-charge carrier generation efficiency (IPCE) of 12%, the power conversion efficiency was less than 1%. A similar study with CdSe incorporating a cobalt (II/III) based redox system, Lee et al. [44] was able to improve the performance of IPCE to 36% as well as the overall power conversion efficiency to 1%. Replacement of TiO2 with semiconducting single-walled carbon nanotubes (SWCNTs), stacked-cup carbon nanotubes (SCCNTs), and fullerene (C60) was studied which demonstrated that nanotubes can capture electrons from CdSe quantum dots [45,46]. Although these inorganic organic hybrid solar cells can be assembled, they failed to give any reportable power conversion efficiency.

Recently, Shu et al. developed a series of CdSexS(1−x) based solar cells using TiO2 as photoelectron acceptor and Na2S as electrolyte by the successive ionic layer adsorption and reaction (SILAR) technique. By varying the ratio of selenide and sulphur, they were able to achieve the overall conversion efficiency of 2.27%. In this study, they prepared core shell quantum dots using CdSexS(1−x)/CdSe and were able to promote the efficiency to 3.17%. Similar studies conducted by Toyoda et al. [48] with CdS/CdSe solar cell using Na2S showed a slightly higher efficiency of 3.5%. Incorporating semiconductor SnO2 with CdS/CdSe solar cell improved the efficiency to 3.68%

. A study with different electrodes based CdS/CdSe solar cells disclosed that mixed CuS/CoS counter electrode can significantly increase the power conversion efficiency to 4.1% than the efficiency of the single electrode employing CuS (3.2%) and CoS (3.8%). However, the performance of the hollow core mesoporous shell carbon (HCMSC) counter electrode using polysulfide electrolyte was comparatively lower (1.08%) than the other electrolytes used in solar cells. Rod like CdSe quantum dots sensitized solar cells using ZnS electrode were reported recently and achieved an efficiency of 2.7% .

In a very recent study, Santra and Kamat claimed to achieve an efficiency of 5.42% for a CdS/CdSe based solar cell fabricated by successive ionic layer adsorption and reaction (SILAR) approach presented in Figure 8. In this study, they used Mn as a dopant since it can modify the electronic and photophysical properties of the quantum dots and can create different electronic states in the intermediate regions. Forming intermediate band gaps can help to reduce the recombination loss of electron from TiO_2 to the valence band of the quantum dots. In this study, it was observed that the absorption peak of the Mn-doped CdS quantum dots was increased to 570 nm (corresponding band gap 2.6 eV) relative to the peak at 520 nm (corresponding band gap 2.4 eV) for undoped CdS.

Although hybrid quantum dots CdS/CdSe shifted the absorption peak further red to 690 nm; however, only a slight difference was observed between Mn-doped and Mn-undoped CdS/CdSe. In comparison with four quantum dots solar cells, the highest incident-photon-to-carrier conversion-efficiency (IPCE) is observed in the Mn-doped CdS/CdSe based solar cell with an enhancement value from 68% to 80%. The other important photovoltaic parameters including short circuit current (Isc), open circuit voltage (Voc), fill factor (FF), and power conversion efficiency (η) of the Mn-doped CdS/Se are 20.7 mA/cm2, 558 mV, 0.47 and 5.42%, respectively.

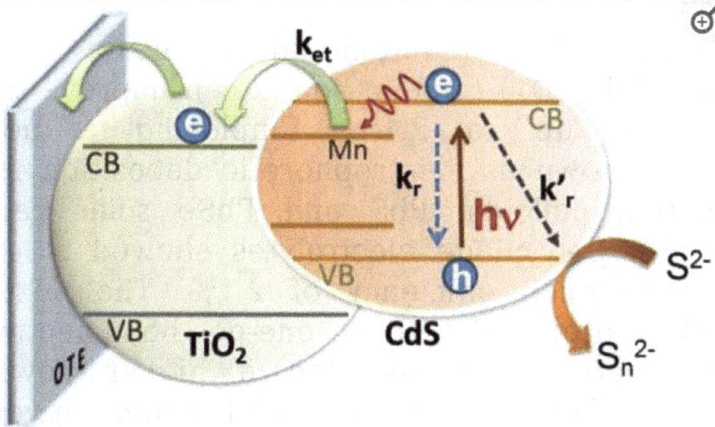

Lead Quantum Dots Based Solar Cells

PbS quantum dot is an ideal material for solar cells which can be used as an electron donor for wide bandgap semiconductors including TiO2 and ZnO. PbS and PbSe quantum dots of group IV-VI have some exceptional properties including (i) efficient light absorbing capacity from visible and near IR regions, (ii) relatively long excitonic life time (200–800 ns), (iii) high quantum efficiency (80%), (iv) comparatively large Bohr radius (18nm of PbS and 46nm of PbSe), (v) water solubility . In an earlier study, Plass et al. showed that the power conversion efficiency of a PbS based heterojunction solar cell (prepared by chemical bath deposition method) incorporating organic charge transport material spiro-OMeTAD was less than 1% (more details about solid-state QDSSCs.

However, PbSe quantum dots using 1,2-ethanedithiol (EDT) organic ligand can improve the performance up to 2.1%. Employing a new technique known as electrophoretic deposition for constructing colloidal PbS and PbSe solar cells linked with polysulfide electrolytes showed a low power conversion efficiency of 2.1%. The mixed PbSxSe1−x prepared with an one-pot hot injection reaction method demonstrated a higher power conversion efficiency of 3.3% which is comparatively higher than the efficiency observed for pure PbS and PbSe QDs based device. By reducing the size to 2.3 nm of PbSe (band gap 1.6 eV) and using a modified one-pot hot injection method, Ma et al. [67] were able to promote the power efficiency to 4.7% with AM1.5 illumination. However, the open circuit voltage of this cell was initially enhanced by increasing the bandgap and the effect diminished earlier than expected. Further reducing the bandgap of colloidal PbS to 1.3 eV increased the average power conversion efficiency to 4.9%, and the champion device achieved an efficiency of 5.1% with Voc = 0.51 V, Isc = 16.2 mA cm−2, and FF = 58%. Recently, for the first time Etgar et al used PbS quantum dots with anatase TiO2 nanosheets incorporating its dominant facet (001) to construct a heterojunciton solar cell using a simple hydrothermal protocol where tetrabutyltitanate and

HF act as precursor and solvent, respectively. Under 0.9 light intensity, this cell achieved a power conversion efficiency of 4.73%.

The Sargent group in Toronto first constructed tandem colloidal quantum dots solar cells where they employed quantum dots having a bandgap of 1.6 eV for covering visible region (front cell) and another quantum dots of 1 eV for the infrared region (back cell) [69]. They used a TiO_2 semiconductor to accept the photoelectron. In order to allow a barrier free transport of electrons from one junction to another junction, they employed a new approach named graded recombination level (GRL) using n-type MoO_3, iridium tin oxide (ITO) and aluminum-doped zinc oxide (AZO).

The highest power conversion efficiency of this two junction solar cell was 4.2%. However, the power conversion efficiency of the individual junction was about 3.0%. The short circuit current (Isc), open circuit voltage (Voc), and fill factor (FF) of the tandem was 8.3 mA cm−2, 1.06 V, and 48%, respectively. Although open circuit voltage of the tandem cell was comparatively higher, the fill factor value was relatively low. The low power efficiency of the tandem may be due to the large antiparticle space between the quantum dots since organic ligands usually create space because of their long chain. Moreover, these organic ligands create insulating barrier between the colloidal quantum dots which eventually block the efficient electron-hole transport. However, some short organic and inorganic ligands can passivate the surface of quantum dots and can densify the films within the solid state. This process is known as "atomic ligand passivation". In a recent study, the Sargent group used inorganic ligands which not only can minimize the interparticle space but also can promote the rapid electron-hole transport by passivating the surface of colloidal PbS QDs as shown in Figure 9. Inorganic halide ligands (Cl−, Br−, I−) lowered the recombination loss which is one of the reasons for lower power conversion efficiency.

This inorganic ligand based colloidal QDs solid state solar cell promoted the power conversion efficiency to 6% which was the highest efficiency found in quantum dots based single solar cells in 2011. In 2012, this group was able to improve the power conversion efficiency (6.6%) of PbS colloidal based all inorganic (homojunction) quantum dots solar cell by introducing a new solution-phase halide passivation technique which promotes high carrier mobility.

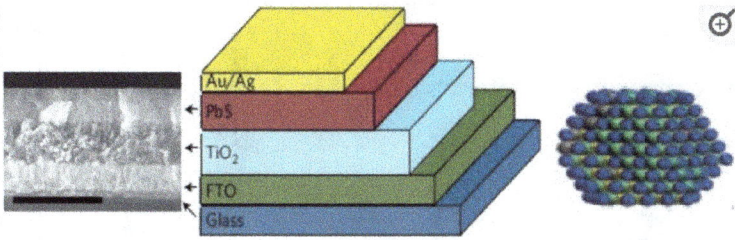

The power conversion efficiency of different solar cells.

Solar cells	Materials	Efficiency
Silicon	Si wafer	15.70%
		22.40%
Dye Sensitized	Ru bipyridine	11.18%

Solar cells	Materials	Efficiency
	Zn porphyrin	12.30%
Solid-State DSC	Z907 dye with spiro-OMeTAD (doctor-blading)	3.00%
	Z907 dye with spiro-OMeTAD	5.65%
	Y123 dye with spiro-OMeTAD and p-type Co(III) dopant	7.20%
Polymer	P3HT, IC60BA, PBDTT-DPP, PC71BM	8.60%

Solar cells	Materials	Efficiency
	Same as above [a]	10.60%
Quantum Dots (Liquid Eletrolytes)	Rod like CdSe	2.70%
	$CdSe_xS_{(1-x)}/CdSe$	3.17%
	CdS/CdSe	3.50%
	CdS/CdSe	3.68%
	CdS/CdSe	4.10%

Solar cells	Materials	Efficiency
	CdS/CdSe	5.42%
	CdS/CdSe Invert Type I	5.32%
	CdSe	5.42%
	PbS/PbSe	2.10%

CHAPTER FIVE

SOLAR POWER IN SMART GRID TECHNOLOGY

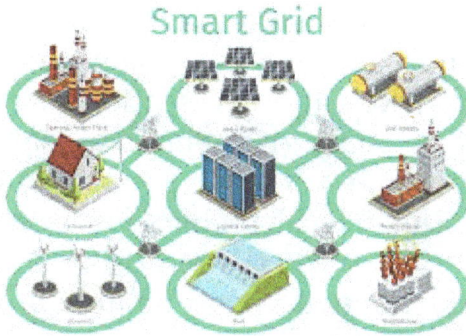

Smart Grid

Energy demand has increased as a result of globalization, rising living standards, and technological advancements. This caused an increase in power usage that, if left untreated, might become unmanageable. This is a concerning issue, not just for the provision of renewable energy but also for the global preservation of the ecosystem. Cities use around 75-80% of global energy consumption, accounting for 80% of greenhouse gas emissions. The power grid is the traditional centralized system of transmission of electrical energy. Traditional power networks are solely concerned with a few fundamental tasks, such as energy production, transmission, and regulation. The current electrical system is unstable, with significant transmission losses, low power quality, a high risk of rolling blackouts, insufficient electricity supply, and many other barriers.

Smart grid technology is revolutionizing the way we generate, distribute, and consume electricity. At the heart of this transformation is the integration of renewable energy sources, such as solar power, into our existing power grids. In this section, we will explore the concept of smart grid technology and its importance in harnessing renewable energy for a sustainable future. Smart grid technology refers to an advanced electrical grid system that utilizes digital communication and automation to optimize the generation, distribution, and consumption of electricity. Unlike traditional power grids, which operate on a one-way flow of electricity from centralized power plants to consumers, smart grids enable bi-directional flow and real-time monitoring of energy usage.

One key aspect of smart grid technology is its ability to integrate renewable energy sources like solar power into the grid. Solar panels convert sunlight into electricity through photovoltaic cells. By connecting these solar panels to the smart grid system, excess electricity generated during peak sunlight hours can be fed back into the grid for others to use. This not only reduces reliance on fossil fuels but also promotes a more decentralized and resilient energy infrastructure.

The importance of incorporating solar power into smart grids cannot be overstated. As concerns about climate change and environmental sustainability grow, transitioning from fossil fuels to renewable energy sources has become imperative. Solar power offers numerous benefits such as reducing greenhouse gas emissions, lowering dependence on finite resources like coal or natural gas, and providing a clean source of energy that does not produce harmful by products.

Furthermore, integrating solar power into smart grids enhances overall system efficiency by reducing transmission losses associated with long-distance electricity transport from large-scale power plants. It also promotes local generation and consumption of clean energy within communities.By embracing this innovative approach to managing our electrical systems, we can reduce carbon emissions while ensuring reliable access to clean and affordable electricity for generations to come.

How Solar Power Integration Enhances the Efficiency and Resilience of Smart Grids

Solar power integration plays a crucial role in enhancing the efficiency and resilience of smart grids. As renewable energy sources become increasingly important in the pursuit of sustainability, solar panels have emerged as a prominent solution for generating clean electricity. When integrated into smart grid systems, solar power offers several benefits that contribute to grid efficiency and reliability. One key advantage of solar power integration is its ability to reduce dependency on traditional fossil fuel-based energy sources. By harnessing the sun's energy, solar panels provide a renewable and environmentally friendly alternative to conventional electricity generation methods. This reduces greenhouse gas emissions and helps combat climate change.

Smart grids utilize advanced technologies such as sensors, meters, and communication networks to monitor and manage electricity flow in real time. By incorporating solar power generation data into this system, grid operators can make informed decisions regarding load balancing, demand response programs, and energy storage management. This results in more efficient utilization of available resources and minimizes wastage.

In addition to improving efficiency, the integration of solar power also enhances the resilience of smart grids. Solar panels generate electricity locally at distributed locations, which reduces reliance on centralized power plants and long-distance transmission lines. This decentralized approach improves grid reliability by mitigating the risk of widespread outages caused by disruptions in transmission infrastructure or natural disasters.

Solar power integration promotes energy independence at both individual and community levels. Homes equipped with rooftop solar panels can generate their own electricity during daylight hours, reducing reliance on external sources for their energy needs. In cases where excess energy is generated, it can be fed back into the grid through net metering programs or stored for later use using battery storage systems. Overall, integrating solar power into smart grids presents numerous advantages for enhancing efficiency and resilience within our electrical infrastructure. By harnessing renewable energy sources like solar panels alongside advanced grid management technologies, we can pave the way towards a more sustainable future.

The Benefits of Solar-Powered Smart Grids for Consumers and Utility Companies

As the world marches steadily towards a greener and more sustainable future, the integration of solar power into smart grid technology stands as a pivotal step in this transformative journey. Smart grids, infused with the power of the sun, offer an array of benefits that extend far beyond the conventional electrical grid. In this section, we will explore the advantages of solar-powered smart grids for both consumers and utility companies.

Cost Savings

For consumers, one of the most tangible advantages of solar-powered smart grids is the potential for substantial cost savings. Traditional energy sources often come with fluctuating prices that can burden households and businesses alike. However, solar power, harnessed and stored intelligently within smart grids, provides a stable and predictable energy source. This stability translates into reduced electricity bills for consumers, making it an economically savvy choice. Utility companies also reap the rewards of solar-powered smart grids through reduced operational costs. The optimization of energy distribution, enabled by smart grid technology, minimizes wastage and inefficiencies. Additionally, the incorporation of solar power allows utility companies to rely less on fossil fuels, reducing fuel procurement and maintenance expenses.

Reduced Carbon Footprint

One of the central themes of our sustainable future is the reduction of greenhouse gas emissions. Solar-powered smart grids play a crucial role in this endeavour. By harnessing the clean and renewable energy of the sun, these grids significantly diminish the carbon footprint associated with traditional energy generation.

Consumers who opt for solar-powered smart grids can take pride in knowing that their energy consumption is eco-friendly. They contribute to the reduction of harmful emissions, thereby helping combat climate change and environmental degradation.Utility companies, too, benefit from a greener image, aligning with the growing demand for sustainable energy sources among environmentally conscious consumers.

The integration of solar power into smart grid technology signifies a significant leap forward in our pursuit of a sustainable future. Consumers enjoy cost savings, reduced environmental impact, and active participation in demand response programs. Utility companies benefit from cost efficiencies and improved grid management. As solar-powered smart grids continue to evolve, they offer a shining example of how renewable energy sources can reshape the way we harness and distribute power.

Overcoming Challenges in Implementing Solar Power into Smart Grid Infrastructure

While the integration of solar power into smart grid technology offers a plethora of benefits, it's not without its unique set of challenges. One of the primary hurdles is the intermittent nature of solar energy generation. Solar power production is contingent on weather conditions and time of day, which can lead to fluctuations in energy supply. However, with strategic planning and innovative solutions, these challenges can be effectively addressed. Here are five essential tips for overcoming these hurdles and ensuring seamless incorporation of solar power into smart grid infrastructure:

Efficient Energy Storage Solutions: One of the key strategies for managing the intermittent nature of solar power is the implementation of efficient energy storage solutions. Energy storage systems, such as advanced batteries, capacitors, and pumped hydro storage, allow excess solar energy to be stored during periods of high generation and released when demand exceeds supply. These systems act as a buffer, ensuring a consistent and reliable energy supply to the grid.

Demand Response Programs: Implementing demand response programs can help balance energy supply and demand effectively. By incentivizing consumers to adjust their energy consumption during peak and off-peak hours, utility companies can better match solar power generation with demand. Smart grid technology enables real-time communication with consumers, allowing them to participate actively in conserving energy during periods of high demand.

Grid Flexibility and Redundancy: Smart grids are designed to be flexible and resilient. Building redundancy into the grid infrastructure ensures that if one part of the system experiences issues, others can compensate. This redundancy minimizes the risk of power outages due to the intermittent nature of solar energy and enhances grid stability.

Predictive Analytics and Forecasting: Leveraging predictive analytics and forecasting tools is vital for optimizing solar power integration into smart grids. These tools use historical data and real-time information to predict solar power generation patterns. Utilities can adjust their grid operations based on these predictions, ensuring that solar energy is utilized efficiently.

Hybrid Systems: Hybrid systems that combine solar power with other renewable energy sources, such as wind or geothermal, can provide a more stable energy supply. By diversifying the energy mix, utilities can reduce the impact of solar power intermittency. Hybrid systems also enable a more consistent generation of renewable energy, even when weather conditions are not ideal for solar.

Integrating solar power into smart grid infrastructure presents unique challenges, however, these obstacles can be overcome through innovative solutions and strategic planning. As technology continues to advance, the synergy between solar power and smart grids will play a pivotal role in our transition to a greener and more sustainable energy landscape.

The Future Outlook:

Advancements and Innovations in Solar-Powered Smart Grid Technology

The role of solar power in smart grid technology is poised for an exciting and transformative future. As our world continues its journey towards a sustainable and renewable energy landscape, solar-powered smart grids are at the forefront of this revolution. In this section, we'll explore the future outlook, highlighting the emerging trends and innovations that will shape the integration of solar energy into smart grids.

Enhanced Energy Storage Solutions: The future of solar-powered smart grids will see significant advancements in energy storage technology. Researchers and engineers are tirelessly working on developing high-capacity, long-lasting batteries and energy storage systems. These innovations will enable solar-generated energy to be stored more efficiently and for more extended periods. With improved storage solutions, the intermittent nature of solar power will become less of a challenge, ensuring a stable and consistent energy supply.

Grid Decentralization and Microgrids: A notable trend on the horizon is the decentralization of power grids. Solar-powered micro grids are gaining popularity, especially in remote or off-grid areas. These self-sustaining energy systems rely heavily on solar power and battery storage, reducing the need for long-distance power transmission. As technology advances, we can expect to see more communities and facilities adopting micro grids as a reliable and sustainable energy source.

Artificial Intelligence and Predictive Analytics: Artificial intelligence (AI) and machine learning are poised to play a pivotal role in the optimization of solar-powered smart grids. AI algorithms can analyze vast amounts of data to predict solar energy generation patterns accurately. This predictive capability will enable utility companies to fine-tune grid operations, matching energy supply with demand more effectively. AI-driven analytics will also contribute to the efficient management of grid resources, reducing waste and enhancing grid stability.

Integration of IoT and Communication Networks: The Internet of Things (IoT) and advanced communication networks will facilitate real-time monitoring and control of smart grids. Smart sensors and devices connected to the grid will provide valuable data on energy consumption, solar power generation, and grid performance. This interconnectedness will empower consumers to make informed decisions about their energy usage, contributing to energy conservation and sustainability.

Grid Resilience and Cybersecurity: As solar-powered smart grids become more prevalent, ensuring grid resilience and cybersecurity will be paramount. The future will witness investments in grid hardening to withstand extreme weather events and cyberattacks. Innovations in grid protection will safeguard the reliability and security of our energy infrastructure.

CHAPTER SIX

HYDROGEN ENERGY

i. As a potential fuel, hydrogen is appealing because it has a high energy density by weight. This results in a 38% efficiency for a combustion engine, compared to 30% when gasoline was used as a fuel. In addition, it provides an environmentally clean source of energy that does not release pollutants.

ii. Hydrogen production is a large and growing industry. Globally, 50 million metric tons of hydrogen (equivalent to 170 million tons of oil) was produced in 2004. There are two primary uses for hydrogen today. Half of the hydrogen produced is used to synthesize ammonia in the Haber process. The other half is used to convert heavy petroleum sources into lighter fractions which can be used as fuels.

iii. Hydrogen is flexible and abundant on earth n very many compounds. It can be produced from a wide variety of resources and can be used in a wide range of applications, such as power generation, as a transport fuel for low carbon vehicles, for the chemical industry, and for low carbon heating.

iv. Hydrogen vehicles retain a number of important advantages:
-They can be rapidly refuelled in just a couple of minutes
-Have a range of many hundreds of kilometres.

v. In addition to transport, hydrogen may also be useful as a way to store renewable energy from intermittent sources for example, when the wind is blowing but there is not high demand for electricity.

vi. Another possibility is to use hydrogen as a heating fuel in our homes and buildings, either blended with natural gas or neat.

ii. Hydrogen is high in energy, yet an engine that burns pure hydrogen produces almost no pollution. For example, NASA uses hydrogen fuel to launch the space shuttles.

1.2. Key facts about Hydrogen gas
• Hydrogen is the most common chemical element in the universe
• It does not exist in nature in its elemental form
• It exists in other chemical compounds (natural gas, biomass, alcohols or water) and can be separated from them.

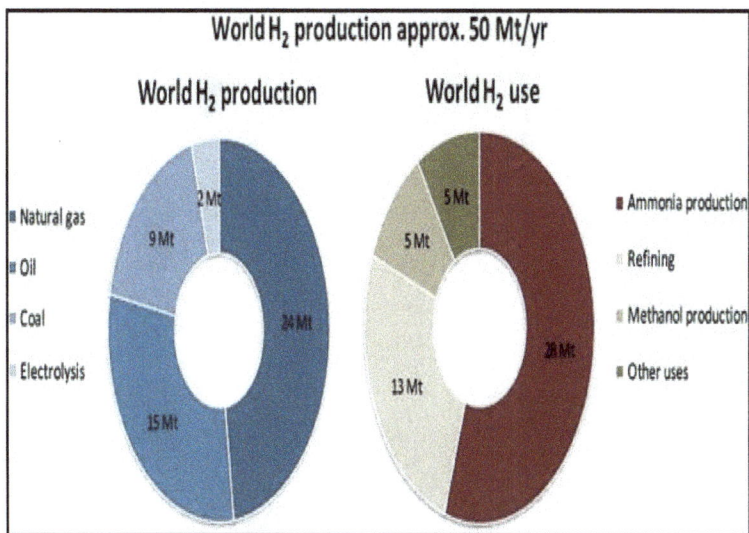

World H$_2$ production approx. 50 Mt/yr

World H$_2$ production

Natural gas
Oil
Coal
Electrolysis

2 Mt
9 Mt
24 Mt
15 Mt

World H$_2$ use

Ammonia production
Refining
Methanol production
Other uses

5 Mt
5 Mt
28 Mt
13 Mt

• As such, hydrogen is not a primary energy source, but an energy carrier.

• Hydrogen is the smallest of all atoms and is the lightest gas

-Other methods for Coal/Biomass use in hydrogen production are Pyrolysis of Biomass, Anaerobic digestion of Biomass and Fermentative Microorganisms of Biomass which require moderate to high steam or heat. They also produce emissions.

-Other methods for Water use in Hydrogen production are Thermal Chemical Water splitting, Photo biological for Water and Algae strains and Photo electrochemical which require high temperature heat from Nuclear energy and Sunlight. They have no emissions but are very expensive.

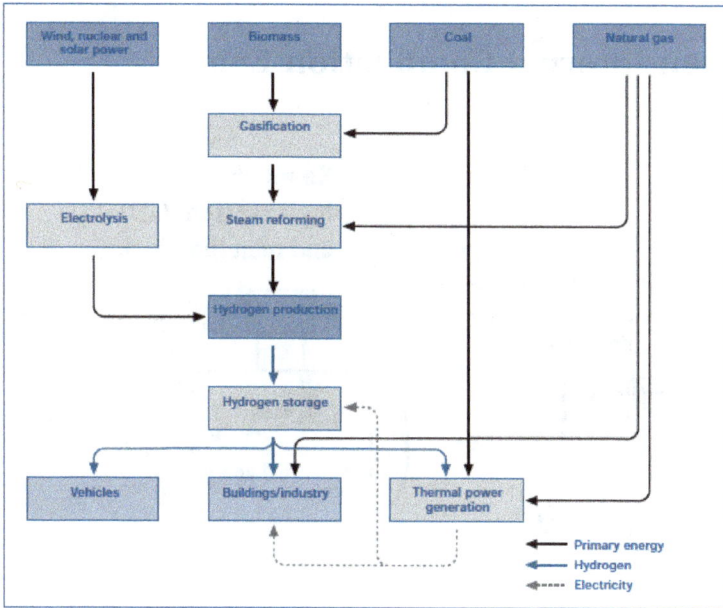

Source: Menecon Consulting analysis.

1. TECHNOLOGIES

Hydrogen can be used as the primary fuel in an internal combustion engine or in a fuel cell.

3.1. Hydrogen in Internal Combustion Engines

A hydrogen internal combustion engine is similar to that of a gasoline engine, where hydrogen combusts with oxygen in the air and produces expanding hot gases that directly move the physical parts of an engine. The only emissions are water vapour and insignificant amounts of nitrous oxides. The efficiency is small, around 20%.

Hydrogen Internal Combustion Engine

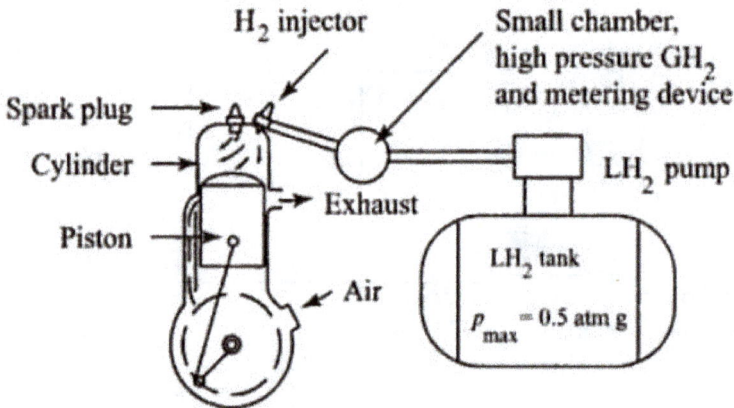

H$_2$ injector

Small chamber, high pressure GH$_2$ and metering device

Spark plug

Cylinder

Piston

Exhaust

Air

LH$_2$ pump

LH$_2$ tank

$p_{max} = 0.5$ atm g

1.2. Fuel Cell Technology

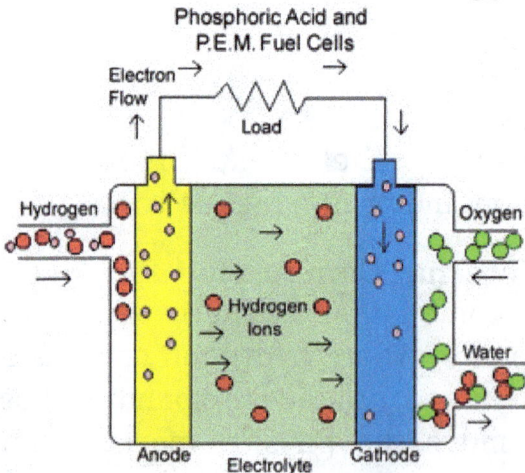

Phosphoric Acid and P.E.M. Fuel Cells

Electron Flow

Load

Hydrogen

Oxygen

Hydrogen Ions

Water

Anode

Electrolyte

Cathode

Fuel cells operate best on pure hydrogen.
A fuel cell combines hydrogen and oxygen to produce electricity, heat, and water. Fuel cells are often compared to batteries. Both convert the energy produced by a chemical reaction into usable electric power. However, the fuel cell will produce electricity as long as fuel (hydrogen) is supplied, never losing its charge.

The use of a fuel cell eliminates the nitrous oxide emissions. Furthermore, the fuel cell is 40-80% efficient.

1.2.1. Applications of the Fuel Cell
1) Storage of renewable energy through a PHOTOVOLTAIC SOLAR HYDROGEN

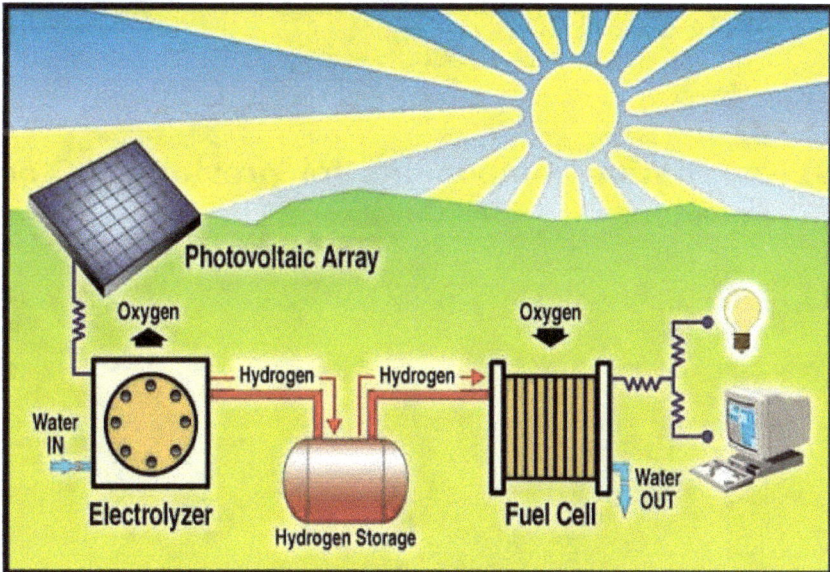

2) Fuel Cell Car

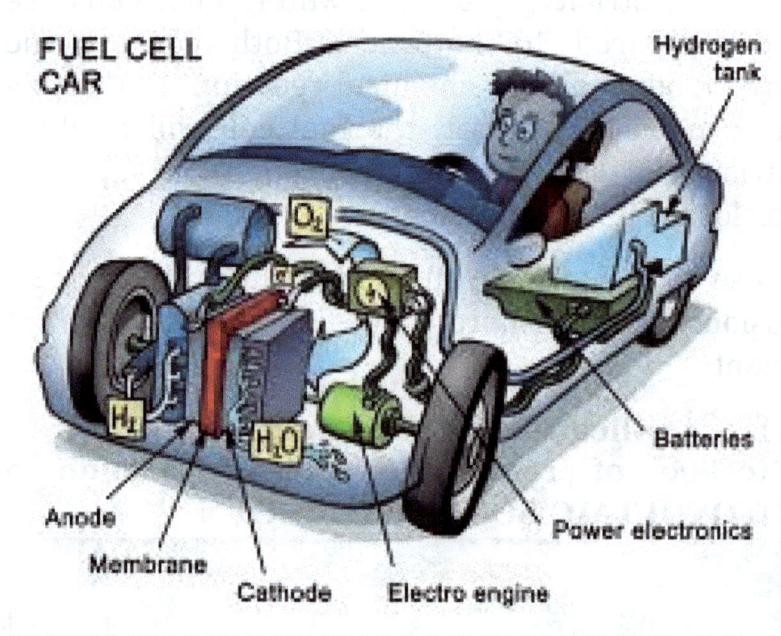

FUEL CELL CAR

Hydrogen tank

O_2

H_2

H_2O

Anode

Membrane

Cathode

Electro engine

Batteries

Power electronics

3) Key System components for providing AC or DC Power

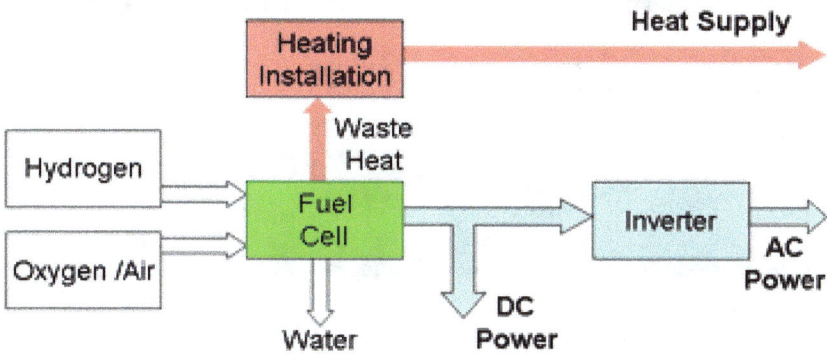

Fuel Cells used in CHP Applications

2. HYDROGEN STORAGE

Developing safe, reliable, compact, and cost-effective hydrogen storage technologies is one of the most technically challenging barriers to the widespread use of hydrogen as a form of energy. Hydrogen is the lightest gas in the entire Universe. One litre of this gas weighs only 90 mg under normal atmospheric pressure, which means that it is 11 times lighter than the air we breathe.

A volume of around 11 m^3 (which is the volume of the trunk of a large utility or commercial vehicle) is needed to store just 1 kg of hydrogen, which is the quantity needed to drive 100 km. For this reason, its density must be increased using one of the following techniques:

153

How is hydrogen stored?

Physical-based

Material-based

Compressed Gas · **Cold/Cryo Compressed** · **Liquid H$_2$**

Adsorbent · **Liquid organic** · **Interstitial hydride** · **Complex hydride** · **Chemical hydrogen**

Ex. MOF-5 · Ex. BN-methyl cyclopentane · Ex. LaNi$_5$H$_6$ · Ex. NaAlH$_4$ · Ex. NH$_3$BH$_3$

  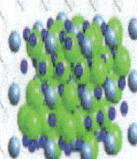 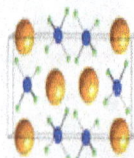 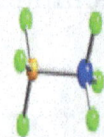

= H$_2$ accessible surface

= H = Al = Na

= H = N = B

4.1. High- pressure storage in the gaseous form

Hydrogen is an ultra-light gas that can be highly compressed to reduce its specific volume. The easiest way to decrease the volume of a gas, at constant temperatures, is to increase its pressure. The main reason for pressurizing hydrogen is that when it is pressurized its apparent volume becomes smaller making storage and transportation convenient. So, at 700 bar, which is 700 times normal atmospheric pressure, hydrogen has a density of 42 kg/m³, compared with 0.090 kg/m³ under normal pressure and temperature conditions. At this pressure, 5 kg of hydrogen can be stored in a 125-liter tank.

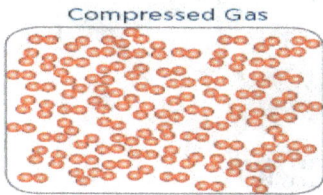

Compressed Gas

Pressurised Vessel

2.2. Liquefaction process

This process uses a very low temperature storage mechanism to store hydrogen in its liquid form. Hydrogen turns into a liquid when it is cooled to a temperature below -250 °C. At -252.8°C and 1.013 Bar, liquid hydrogen has a density of close to 71 kg/m³. At this pressure, 5 kg of hydrogen can be stored in a 75-liter tank.

The simplest liquefaction process is the Linde cycle or Joule-Thompson expansion cycle. In this process,

155

the gas is compressed at ambient pressure, then
cooled in a heat exchanger, before passing through
a throttle valve where it undergoes an isenthalpic
Joule-Thompson expansion, producing some liquid.
This liquid is removed and the cool gas is returned
to the compressor via the heat exchanger.

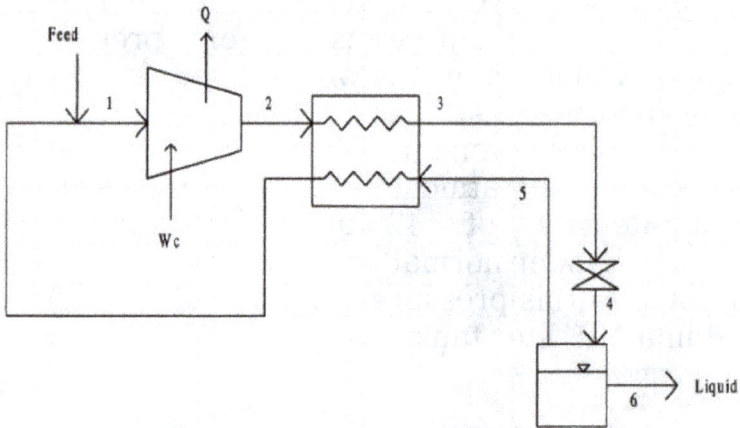

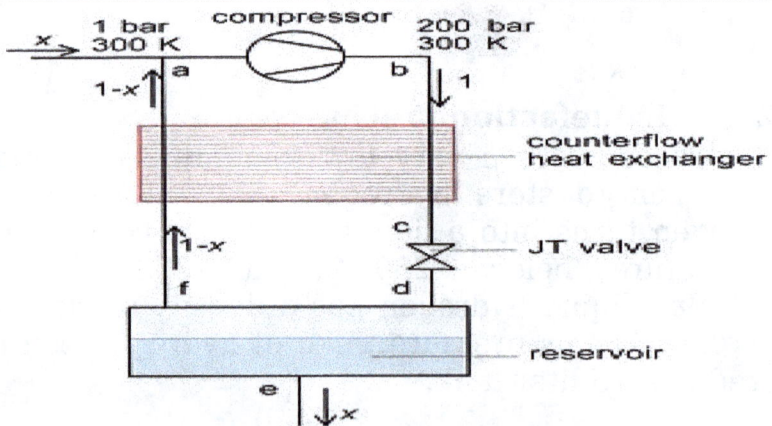

4.3. Hydride-based storage in the solid form

The methods used to store hydrogen in the solid form involve techniques that bring into play the mechanisms of absorption or adsorption of hydrogen by a material. One example is to form solid metallic hydrides through the reaction of hydrogen with certain metal alloys.

4.3.1. in adsorption

Hydrogen attaches to the surface of a material either as hydrogen molecules (H2) or hydrogen atoms (H).

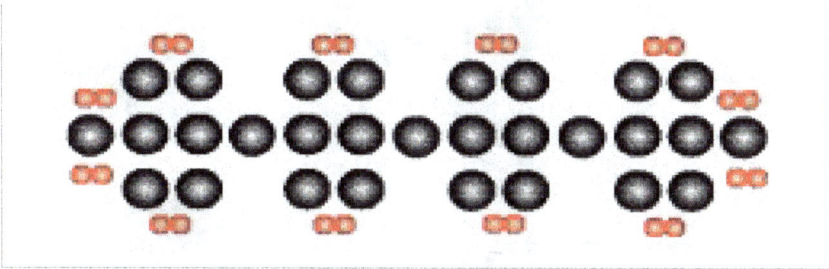

4.3.2. In absorption

Hydrogen molecules dissociate into hydrogen atoms that are incorporated into the solid lattice framework – this method may make it possible to store larger quantities of hydrogen in smaller volumes at low pressure and at temperatures close to room temperature.

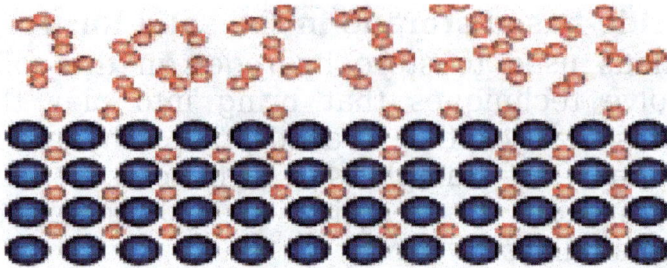

Finally, hydrogen can be strongly bound within molecular structures, as chemical compounds containing hydrogen atoms.

The most common metal hydrides

Metal	Hydride
Pd	$PdH_{0.6}$
$LaNi_5$	$LaNi_5H_6$
ZrV_2	$ZrV_2H_{5.5}$
FeTi	$FeTiH_2$
Mg_2Ni	Mg_2NiH_4
TiV_2	TiV_2H_4

4.4. Advantage and Disadvantage of the three hydrogen storage methods

Storage Form	Advantages	Disadvantages
Compressed Gas	Reliable Indefinite storage time Easy to use	Higher capital & operating costs Heat can cause container rupture
Liquid	High density at low pressure	High cost Low temperatures needed Escape can cause fire or asphyxiation
Metal Hydride	High volume efficiencies Easy recovery Very safe	Expensive materials Heavy storage tanks

3. DELIVERY OF HYDROGEN

5.1. Road Delivery of Hydrogen

A hydrogen economy also involves hydrogen transport by trucks and ships. There are other options for hydrogen distribution, but road transport will always play a role, be it to serve remote locations or to provide back-up fuel to filling stations at times of peak demand. Transport by truck, rail or ship is more expensive than gas piping.

3.2. Pipeline Delivery of Hydrogen

Hydrogen pipelines exist, but they are used to transport a chemical commodity from one to another production site. The energy required to move the gas has little is irrelevant, because energy consumption is part of the production costs. This is not so for hydrogen energy transport through pipelines. Gaseous hydrogen can be transported through pipelines much the way natural gas is today. Approximately 1,500 miles of hydrogen pipelines are currently operating in the United States. Owned by merchant hydrogen producers, these pipelines are located where large hydrogen users, such as petroleum refineries and chemical plants, are concentrated such as the Gulf Coast region. Normally, pumps are installed at regular intervals to keep the gas moving. These pumps are energized by energy taken from the delivery stream. The energy required to pump H2 through pipelines is some 4.5 times higher than for natural gas per unit of delivered energy. As a consequence, long distances H2 transportation for energy use may not be economically competitive

4. CARBON CAPTURE AND STORAGE

The prospects for the hydrogen economy becoming a reality in the foreseeable future hinge on advances in carbon capture and storage (CCS) technology, and its integration into hydrogen production based on fossil fuels. This is a necessary, but not a sufficient, condition. Success in deploying CCS would also pave way for environmentally acceptable production of electricity using fossil fuels. However, sequencing technology for carbon adds to the overall cost of producing hydrogen, rather than a direct consumption of the fossil fuel.

There are three distinct steps involved in CCS associated with hydrogen production:

• Capturing CO_2 from the flue-gas streams emitted during the production process (pre-combustion capture).

• Transporting the captured CO_2 by pipeline or in tankers.

• Storing CO_2 underground in deep saline aquifers, depleted oil and gas reservoirs or un mineable coal seams.

5. KEY PLAYERS IN THE RESEARCH AND DEVELOPMENT OF THE HYDROGEN ECONOMY

A growing number of countries have committed to accelerate the development of hydrogen and fuel cell technologies in order to improve their energy, environment and economic security. For example, those countries that have made commitments include:

• The United States has committed $1.7 billion for the first five years of a long-term hydrogen infrastructure, fuel cells, and hybrid vehicle technologies development program.

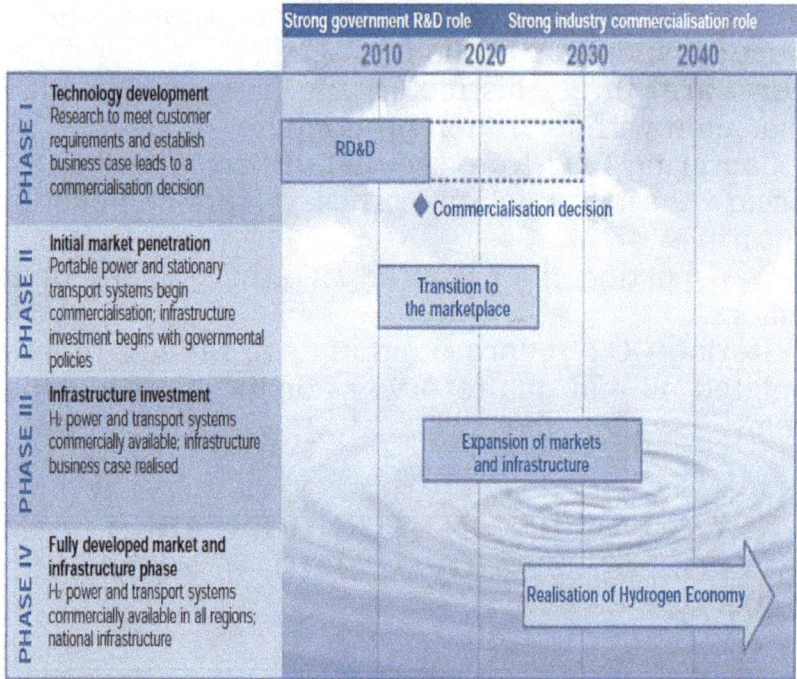

Figure: Transition to the Hydrogen Economy Envisaged by the US Hydrogen Programme

• **The European Union** has committed up to 2 billion Euros over five years to conduct research and development of renewable and hydrogen energy technologies. This effort is complemented by a hydrogen fuel cell bus demonstration program in nine cities.

• **Japan** was the first country to undertake a large-scale hydrogen fuel cell R&D programme – a ten-year, ¥18 billion ($165 million) effort that was completed in 2002. The New Hydrogen Project

162

(NEP), which started up in 2003, focuses on commercialisation. Funding has been raised each year since the project began, reaching ¥35 billion ($320 million) in the financial year 2005. The Japanese government is confident that, with continuing strong financial support, hydrogen fuel cells can become competitive within the next two decades. The NEP sets ambitious targets for the introduction of fuel-cell vehicles, refuelling stations and stationary fuel-cell capacity for 2010 and 2020 (Table).

Table: Hydrogen Commercialisation Targets in Japan

	2010	2020
Fuel-cell vehicles on the road (number)	50,000	5,000,000
Hydrogen refuelling stations (number)	-	4000
Stationary fuel-cell co-generation systems (MW)	2200	10,000

Source: International Energy Agency (2004a).

Other Programmes include;

• ***Australia's*** hydrogen programme is aimed at reducing the carbon/greenhouse gas intensity of energy supply and use, to allow the continued exploitation of its large fossil-fuel reserves. One focus of R&D is the production of hydrogen through the gasification of coal under the COAL21 programme.

• **Canada's** hydrogen R&D focuses on production of hydrogen from renewable energy and fuel cells. Notable successes include the development of the Ballard PEM fuel cell, which led to the world's first demonstration of a fuel-cell bus in 1993, and the Hydrogenics alkaline water electrolyser. Public funding has been running at over C$30 million (US$25 million) per year and cumulative spending since the early 1980s exceeds C$200 million.

• In **France,** hydrogen activities cover PEM and solid-oxide fuel cells; production technologies based on coal-gasification with carbon capture, high-temperature solar and nuclear energy, and small biomass and fossil-fuel reforming; and storage devices. Total annual government spending, including EU contributions, is estimated at about €40 million ($48 million).

• **Germany** is a world leader in hydrogen and fuel cell development. Fuel cells have become the main focus of public and private R&D and demonstration, reflecting in large part the country's traditional strength in car manufacturing. There are a number of demonstration projects under way, including two hydrogen-refuelling stations at Munich Airport to support three buses and a fleet of hydrogen-powered BMWs, and the Clean Energy Partnership initiative in Berlin, which involves the installation of a refuelling station for up to 30 fuel-cell cars. In fact,

164

nearly three-quarters of the fuel cells being demonstrated in Europe are in Germany. In total, the country's fuel-cell industry employs an estimated 3000 people. Total public funding for hydrogen-related activities is estimated at €34 million ($41 million) per year

• The other OECD countries with hydro economy commitments are Italy and Korea. Outside the OECD, the leading countries in hydrogen R&D are **China, India, Russia and Brazil.** *China's* hydrogen R&D and demonstration efforts are motivated largely by severe pollution in many of its cities, as well as by worries about energy security. Annual public funding is thought to be in the tens of millions of dollars, with even larger sums being spent by private organisations.

.

Table 1: Public Research and Development Spending on Hydrogen and Other Energy Technologies in the Largest OECD Countries, 2003 ($ million)

	Hydrogen	Fossil fuels	Renewables	Nuclear	Other	Total
Canada*	24	47	30	47	92	240
Japan	270	n.a.	n.a.	n.a.	n.a.	n.a.
Germany*	34	14	74	154	25	301
France**	45	33	27	359	0	463
Italy	34	15	61	107	124	341
United Kingdom	3	5	20	n.a.	n.a.	n.a.
United States*	97	416	243	371	1623	2750

*Federal spending only. ** 2002 data.*

Source: International Energy Agency (2004d).

6. SUPPORT FOR THE HYDROGEN ECONOMY

These commitments demonstrate that many countries share a common interest in advanced research and development that will support the deployment of hydrogen and fuel cell technologies. International cooperation is vital to efficiently achieve national hydrogen and fuel cell technology program goals, for both transportation systems and stationary applications. Building a safe and efficient world-wide infrastructure for hydrogen production, storage, transport, distribution and use is a

166

multinational task that requires careful planning and cooperation. The establishment of International Partnerships for the Hydrogen Economy is a mechanism to organize and implement effective, efficient and focused research, development and deployment programs that advance hydrogen and fuel cell programs

The ultimate goal of the International Partnership for the Hydrogen Economy is that a participating country's consumers will have the practical option of purchasing a competitively price hydrogen powered vehicle and be able to refuel it near their homes and places of work.

The International Partnerships for the Hydrogen Economy will be successful if the following factors characterize the world's transportation sector:
• Hydrogen powered vehicles are competitive with conventional vehicles.
• The price and availability of hydrogen are competitive with conventional fuels.
• Hydrogen fuel is conveniently available to hydrogen vehicle drivers, based on improved fuelling and storage infrastructure.
• Hydrogen energy storage technologies will allow personal transportation systems to operate at the same levels of safety, performance and range as today's gasoline powered vehicles.
• An internationally consistent system of safety codes and standards related to hydrogen utilization is developed and adopted.

7. FEASIBILITY OF A HYDROGEN ECONOMY IN DEVELOPING COUNTRIES

Developing economies have at least as much to gain from a move towards the hydrogen economy as industrialised ones, since they generally suffer more from pollution and their economies tend to be more energy intensive. Yet the transition will probably start later in most developing nations, as they are less able to afford to participate in R&D and the financial incentives needed to kick-start the process. The rich world must be ready to support developing economies in making this happen, as and when it becomes a viable energy solution, to the benefit of the overall push for hydrogen. International and non-governmental organisations have an important role to play in assisting countries in creating a market based policy environment within which hydrogen and other emerging energy technologies are able to compete against existing, conventional energy systems.

Hydrogen economy is undergoing serious consideration in **South African**, in an effort to develop safe, clean and reliable alternative energy sources to fossil fuels. A strong driving force behind this technology is the prevalence of platinum reserves found in South Africa. Platinum. Platinum Group Metals (PGMs) are the key catalytic materials used in most fuel cells, and with more than 75% of the world's known platinum reserves found within the country's borders, there is great potential for socio-economic benefits to be obtained from these natural resources. Currently, there are R&D

institutions working on the production of hydrogen and actualization of the economy, the country also aims at exporting the produced fuel on the long term but at presently investment in the sector is low (R 5million per annum). **Zimbabwe** is also another African country with significant amount of world's platinum resource which could be used in hydrogen production.

8. DISADVANTAGES/ISSUES WITH A HYDROGEN ECONOMY

The two key issues of a source and sustainable energy future are harvesting energy from renewable sources and finding the highest energy efficiency from source to service. Hydrogen process translates to electricity from hydrogen and fuel cells costing at least four times as much as electricity from the grid. In fact, electricity would be much more efficiently used if it were sent directly to the appliances instead. If the original electricity could be directly supplied by wires, as much as 90% could be used in applications.

As a result, hydrogen economy is considered a wasteful economy by some researchers. Their reasons are highlighted below:

- Hydrogen is not a primary energy source, but an energy carrier.
- Large amount of energy required
-To isolate hydrogen from natural compounds (water, natural gas, biomass)
-To package the light gas by compression or liquefaction
-Transfer the energy carrier to the user
- Energy lost when it is converted to useful electricity with fuel cells, which leaves around 25% for practical use
- Lastly, achieving a hydrogen economy is a very costly one. The cost of producing and delivering Hydrogen from natural gas, or producing Hydrogen onsite at a local filling station, is $4 to $5 per Kg (excluding fuel taxes), comparable to a gasoline price of $4 to $5 a gallon. (A Kg of hydrogen contains about the same useable energy as a gallon of gasoline)
- Hence, there is no commercial readiness of hydrogen fuel and its applications e.g. hydrogen cell cars.

Overall, more energy is needed to isolate hydrogen from natural compounds than can ever be recovered from its use and the technologies are still underdeveloped at the moment.

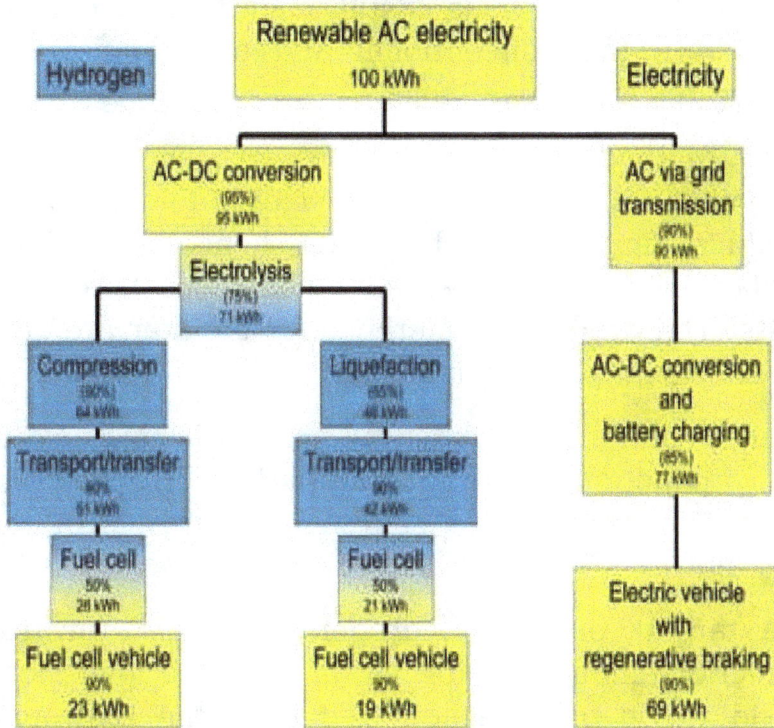

Figure: Comparison in the use of hydrogen fuel and conventional fuel

9. CONCLUSION

There is definitely a potential of having Hydrogen as an energy source, however, the harvesting and getting it ready for use is still much more expensive than both the conventional and other renewable energy resources available.

The Methods of Hydrogen production from Conventional resources (the most dominant) all produce emissions such as CO_2 hence a need for Carbon sequestration which would raise the overall costs. The production methods from water are very expensive and energy intensive.

There is still a lot of research needed in this field in the production, storage and use of hydrogen to make it a competitive source of energy with the existing.

The targets of the "Hydrogen Economy" towards reduction/elimination of a carbon free emissions world would only be achieved if all the Hydrogen was produced from Water, and Renewable energies were the only sources of energy.

While hydrogen can help to decarbonise our energy system, however, it is important to be specific about where and when hydrogen can help. In that sense, it might be better to think about **'hydrogen in the economy'** rather than **'a hydrogen economy'** as such.

CHAPTER SEVEN

POWER TO GAS

1.0   Basic Concept of Power to Gas

The change in the supply structure for energy is mainly driven by the imminent climate change. The energy supply of the future will implement renewable sources at least to a greater extent as today. Beyond any controversy, increasing portions of renewable energy, particularly wind and solar power, already cause local discrepancies between supply and demand in the power grid. There are several possibilities to approach the challenges of a changing energy system. For the time being, the extension of the power grid, load management and energy storage facilities are possible measures to meet the requirements of renewable energies. In terms of storage systems, also seasonal storage possibilities are needed. One promising option for long-term storage is the conversion of renewable electricity to chemical energy carriers, like hydrogen, methane, methanol, formic acid, fuels or the hydrogenation of aromatic hydrocarbons.

The Power-to-Gas technology, one of the chemical storage options among this cited above. The concept based on a conversion of electrical power to a

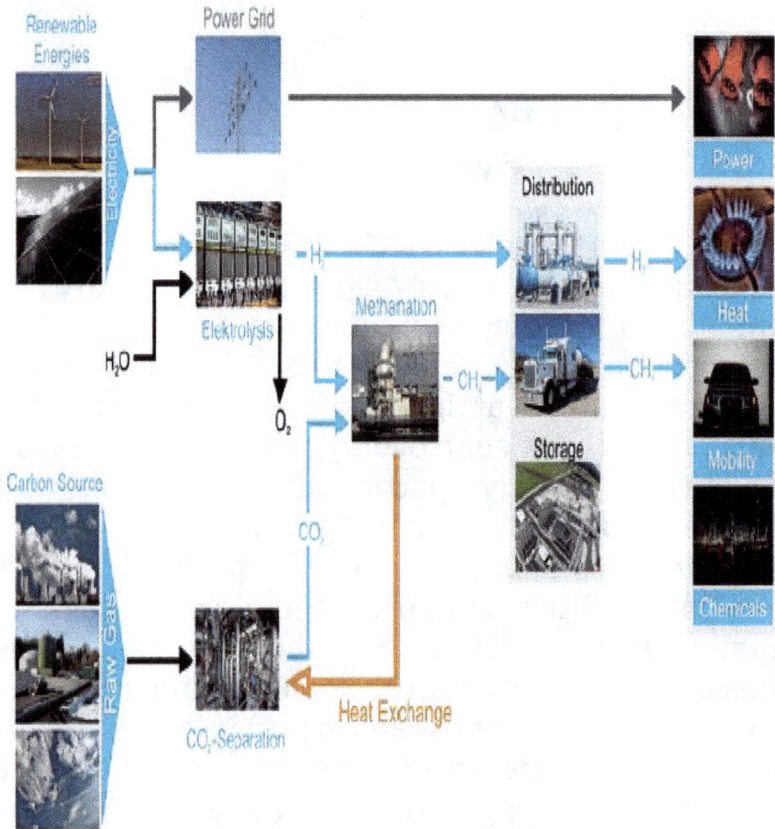

gaseous chemical storage medium, the energy-rich gases hydrogen (H2) and methane (CH4), respectively.

Fig.1 Power to gas concept

In this Fig.1 the renewable electric power is then used in a water electrolysis plant to produce hydrogen and oxygen from water. Oxygen can be released to the atmosphere, or can be preferably used in industrial production processes, like the chemical or the metallurgical industry. But, the utilization of oxygen depends strongly on the local conditions, particularly the distance to the potential consumers and the consumer demand. The actual product is hydrogen which can be transported either in an own hydrogen distribution grid, as admixture in the natural gas grid, by truck or by train. Hydrogen can also be stored in appropriate facilities or together with natural gas in existing natural gas storage infrastructure. Hydrogen is then re-transferred either to electric power, as fuel in the mobility sector, or as valuable feedstock for industry. Particularly, the chemical, petrochemical and metallurgical industries consume huge annual amounts of hydrogen (approximately 600 billion m3/a) which are currently produced mainly by methane steam reforming. Thus, hydrogen is the first possible end-product of the Power-to-Gas process chain. But, the producible volume of hydrogen is limited by either missing hydrogen infrastructure (i.e. hydrogen grid, storage facilities, end-use technologies), or by a maximum allowable content in the natural gas grid. Therefore, the second, but optional process step within the Power-to-Gas process chain is methanation. Hydrogen and carbon dioxide (CO_2) synthesize to methane, either by a chemically or biologically catalyzed reaction. The produced methane is called synthetic or substitute natural gas. The by-product of this reaction is steam (H_2O). The necessary carbon dioxide can be derived from exhaust or process gases of industrial production processes or fossil power plants, biogas plants, or in principal also from the atmosphere or from sea water. The latter options are certainly energy-intensive. Since pure carbon dioxide sources are only rarely available, carbon capture plays a significant role in the Power-to-gas concept, both technically and economically. The main advantage of methane as end-product of the Power-to-Gas process chain is its unlimited usability in the gas infrastructure [1].

Beside the conversion into electricity in combined cycle plants, the utilization as fuel in mobility or as feedstock for industry, substitute natural gas can be also used for heating. The physical and chemical properties of Substitute natural gas are so similar that no technical changes in the end-use systems have to be undertaken. Almost no new investments in infrastructure for transport, storage and utilization are necessary. The conversion to the energy-rich gases hydrogen and methane, respectively, enables the transport of the renewable energy outside the power grid, and also the large scale, long-term storage of renewable energy. The chemical energy carriers can be reconverted to electricity, but a multitude of other utilization routes are possible which result in different efficiencies of the total system [1].

2.0   Conversion Technologies

The key technology for the power to gas concept is electrolysis as it is based on the conversion of electricity to chemical energy carriers during peak power production, and the gas produced from this could be hydrogen or methane if succeeded by Sabatier reaction. Electrolysis is the splitting of water into hydrogen and oxygen where the produced hydrogen can be fed into the natural gas grid, in fuel cell powered cars or used in Sabatier reaction for the production of methane and this can be utilised for electricity generation in future.

2.1 Water Electrolysis

By applying an electric potential to two electrodes, water is split into its components hydrogen and oxygen, which are formed at the cathode and anode, respectively. In addition to the two electrodes, an electrolyser is composed of an electrolyte, which is capable of conducting ions, and a diaphragm, which is an electric isolator and keeps the evolving gas streams separate in order to avoid a flammable mixture. Electrolysers in power-to-gas applications have special requirements:

• High efficiency to avoid unnecessary energy losses
• Highly dynamic behaviour to follow the fluctuating power input of renewables

- Ideally, the ability to produce hydrogen at elevated pressure to reduce energy demand and investment costs for compressors
- Long lifetime and low investment costs to allow for cheap hydrogen production

Three different electrolysis technologies are of interest for PtG process chains: alkaline electrolysis (AEL), polymer electrolyte membranes (PEM), and solid oxide electrolysis (SOEC).

2.1.1 Alkaline Water Electrolysis

The electrolyte consists of aqueous potassium hydroxide with a concentration of 20-40wt% KOH [2] and conducts OH$^-$ ions. The electrodes are made of perforated steel with catalysts based on nickel, cobalt or iron. They are separated by a highly insulating diaphragm. Typical operating temperatures are around 80°C with relatively low

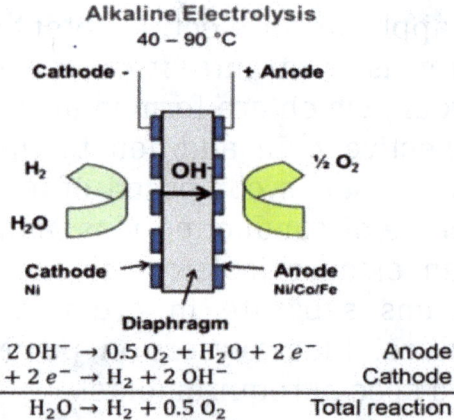

Alkaline Electrolysis
40 – 90 °C

Cathode -   + Anode

H$_2$ OH   ½ O$_2$

H$_2$O

Cathode   Anode
Ni   Ni/Co/Fe

Diaphragm

$2\,OH^- \rightarrow 0.5\,O_2 + H_2O + 2\,e^-$	Anode
$2\,H_2O + 2\,e^- \rightarrow H_2 + 2\,OH^-$	Cathode
$H_2O \rightarrow H_2 + 0.5\,O_2$	Total reaction

current densities of 0.2 -0.4A/cm^2[2]. Most efficient electrolysers achieve stack efficiencies up to 67% (based on LHV of the H$_2$ produced)

178

Fig.2

2.1.2 Proton Exchange Electrolysis

The technology is based on the utilization of a proton-conducting polymeric membrane as the electrolyte and diaphragm combined in one element. The membrane is directly connected to the electrodes in the membrane electrode assembly (MEA). Operating temperatures are limited to about 80°C due to the polymeric material. Hydrogen can be produced at pressures up to 100bar, while it is possible to simultaneously produce the oxygen at atmospheric pressure, thus avoiding the safety issue of handling pressurized oxygen and also increasing efficiency. The cell efficiency is of the same magnitude as that of alkaline electrolysers, but stack

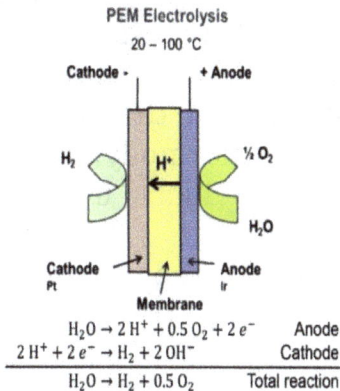

PEM Electrolysis
20 – 100 °C

Cathode -   + Anode

H_2 H^+ $\frac{1}{2}O_2$

H_2O

Cathode   Anode
Pt   Ir

Membrane

$H_2O \rightarrow 2\,H^+ + 0.5\,O_2 + 2\,e^-$	Anode
$2\,H^+ + 2\,e^- \rightarrow H_2 + 2\,OH^-$	Cathode
$H_2O \rightarrow H_2 + 0.5\,O_2$	Total reaction

179

efficiency is lower. This effect will be minimized when PEM electrolysers reach the same sizes as alkaline electrolysers [3]. Major issues concerning PEM electrolysers are related to the costs. The required noble catalysts (Pt, Ir, Ru) and the need for titanium-based bipolar plates lead to current investment costs of about €2000/ kW$_{el}$.

Fig.3

2.1.3 High Temperature Water Electrolysis (Solid Oxide Electrolysis Cell SOEC)

The electrolyte is a solid oxide (solid oxide electrolysis cell, SOEC), which usually consists of O^{2-} conducting yttria-stabilized zirconium oxide. The cell is operated at temperatures of about 700 - 1000°C with steam instead of liquid water and it functions using the reverse process of the solid oxide fuel cell [2]. The unique potential of the SOEC is the thermodynamic effect, which occurs when the water-splitting reaction is

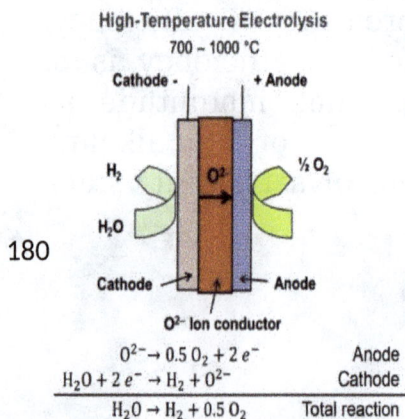

High-Temperature Electrolysis
700 – 1000 °C

Cathode -   + Anode

H_2

O^{2-}

½ O_2

H_2O

180

Cathode   Anode

O^{2-} Ion conductor

$O^{2-} \rightarrow 0.5\,O_2 + 2\,e^-$	Anode
$H_2O + 2\,e^- \rightarrow H_2 + O^{2-}$	Cathode
$H_2O \rightarrow H_2 + 0.5\,O_2$	Total reaction

carried out at elevated temperatures. Here, only part of the total amount of required enthalpy has to be supplied in the form of electric energy. The rest can be provided by a high temperature heat [3].

Fig.4

The electric efficiency, as the ratio of chemically bound energy output to electric input, can therefore even exceed 100% [4,5]. Due to the high temperatures, the SOEC can also be utilized for co-electrolysis, where the reactions of CO_2 to CO and H_2O to H_2 take place simultaneously, thus leading to the production of syngas [5]. This process can be used for the CO_2-neutral production of all kinds of hydrocarbons in the chemical industry. Since this technology is still at an early development stage, many characteristics have to be investigated and improved, such as total system development, part-load behaviour and long-term stability. In general, typical applications for the SOEC are seen in combination with processes which can provide the required heat for the reaction. Additionally, constant operation is preferable, since ceramics are susceptible to thermal stress. This will be a critical issue when the SOEC is used for power-to-gas, since the necessary flexible mode of operation requires numerous start-up and shut-down processes.

	Alkaline electrolysis		PEM electrolysis	
	Today	Potential	Today	Potential
System efficiency [% (LHV)]	<67%	<70%	<67%	<74%
Minimum part load [%PN]	20–40%	10–20%	5–10%	0–5%
Load change [%PN/s]	<10%/s	<25%/s	10–100%/s	10-100 %/s
Operating pressure [bar]	<30	<60	<30	<100
Stack lifetime [h]	~75,000	~95,000	~30,000	~80,000
Investment costs [€/kW$_{el}$]	~1000	~500	~2000	~500

Table 1: Comparison of different electrolyser technologies

	AEC	PEMEC	SOEC
Ions electrolyte	OH^-	H^+	O^{2-}
Current density (A/cm^2)	<0.5	>1	<0.3
Cell voltage (V)	>1.9	>1.8	>1
Temperature (°C)	60–80	60–80	700–1,000
Operating pressure (bar)	<30	<200	<25
(Voltage) Efficiency (%)	60–80	65–80	–
Spec. el. energy consumption (kWh/scbm)	>4.6	>4.8	<3.2
Lower partial load range [% of nominal load (NL)]	30–40	0–10	–
Overload (% of NL)	<150	<200	–
Capacity (scbm H_2)	<760	<40	<5
Cell area (m^2)	<4	<0.3	<0.01

scbm standard cubicmeter

Table 2: Comparison of other parameters for the three water electrolysis technologies

2.2 Methanation of Hydrogen

The Power to Gas Methane method is to combine hydrogen from an electrolyzer with carbon dioxide and convert the two gases to methane using a methanation reaction such as the Sabatier reaction or biological methanation resulting in an extra energy conversion loss of 8%, the methane may then be fed into the natural gas grid if the purity requirement is reached.

2.2.1 Catalytic conversion through the Sabatier Reaction

The Sabatier reaction was discovered in 1902, and is described by

$$CO\ (g) + 3H_2\ (g) \rightarrow CH_4\ (g) + H_2O\ (g) \quad = -206.2\ kJ/mol \quad (1)$$

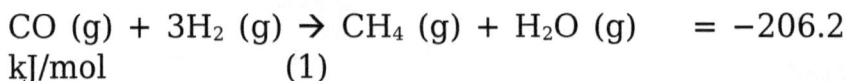

In combination with the shift conversion

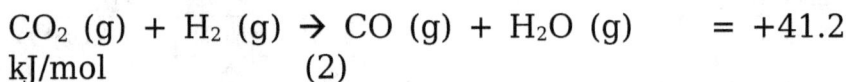

$$CO_2\ (g) + H_2\ (g) \rightarrow CO\ (g) + H_2O\ (g) \quad = +41.2\ kJ/mol \quad (2)$$

a formulation for the reaction of CO2 with hydrogen can be given

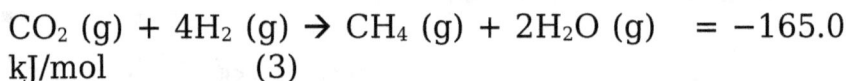

$$CO_2\ (g) + 4H_2\ (g) \rightarrow CH_4\ (g) + 2H_2O\ (g) \quad = -165.0\ kJ/mol \quad (3)$$

Reaction enthalpies in equations are given for a temperature of 25 °C. CO_2 methanation is achieved by the intermediate conversion to CO. Reactions (1) and (3) are strongly exothermic, and all are equilibrium reactions. Lower temperatures result in significantly higher equilibrium constants, and therefore in better conversion rates. But lower temperatures cause unfavorable reaction kinetics, hence appropriate catalysts are used. Due to the volume reduction of the chemical reaction [Eq. 3)], higher pressures basically support better conversion rates. The product gas leaving the reactor contains steam, CO and unconverted educts beside the product CH_4. The product composition can be influenced by the methanation process concept, the reaction parameters and also by the reactor types used. Additionally, the applied catalyst influences kinetics, conversion rate and selectivity of the process. Catalytic active substances for the

184

hydrogenation of CO_2 or CO are group VIII metals, i.e. the Fe-group, the Co-group and the Ni-group [20]. Mainly due to the reasonable cost and satisfactory performance in terms of conversion rates and selectivity, Ni based catalysts are widely utilized for methanation processes today.

2.2.2 Microbial methanation

The above described chemical processes and routes can be substituted by bio-catalysts (enzymes) where the methanation of hydrogen and carbon dioxide is carried out in a biological system. Methanogenic bacteria, which belong to the domain of Archaea, produce the necessary enzymes. Biological methanation is particularly known in biogas processes in which two main reaction paths can be distinguished

Acetoclastic Methanogenesis

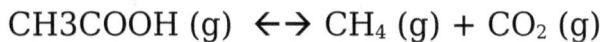

$$CH3COOH \text{ (g)} \leftrightarrow CH_4 \text{ (g)} + CO_2 \text{ (g)}$$

Hydrogenotrophic Methanogenesis

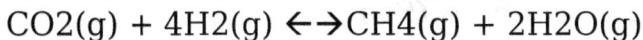

$$CO2(g) + 4H2(g) \leftrightarrow CH4(g) + 2H2O(g)$$

Hydrogen is used as co-substrate in addition to manure or sewage sludge. Hydrogen conversion rates of 80 % are reported which depend on the hydrogen partial pressure and the mixing intensity. The control of the pH value in the system and an instantaneous conversion of the hydrogen to methane seem to be crucial for a stable operation of the process. The selective methanation utilizes adapted microbes under optimized process

185

conditions in a bioreactor. It can be linked to a biogas process, but a self-sustaining operation is also possible which then needs beside the hydrogen an own carbon source. This microbial power-to-gas reaction occurs at ambient conditions, i.e. room temperature and pH 7, at efficiencies that routinely reach 80-100%. However, methane is formed more slowly than in the Sabatier reaction due to the lower temperatures. A direct conversion of CO_2 to methane has also been postulated, circumventing the need for hydrogen production. Microorganisms involved in the microbial power-to-gas reaction are typically members of the order *Methanobacteriales*. Genera that were shown to catalyze this reaction are *Methanobacterium*, *Methanobrevibacter*, and *Methanothermobacter* (thermophile).

3.0 Storage (Gas Infrastructure) and Applications

3.1 Gas Infrastructure (Storage)
Hydrogen or methane produced on large scale can either be stored or distributed using the existing gas infrastructures like the Natural gas grids. For high energy density different types of underground storage can be used.

3.1.1 Underground gas storage
Suitable formations for underground gas storage include the porous rock structures and the man-made caverns in salt rock. Both storage types are

already used worldwide to store gas and oil reserves.

Porous rock storage includes depleted oil & gas fields, and Aquifers. Depleted oil & gas fields have large storage capacity, and their gas tightness, storage suitability and working parameters have already been tested during the extraction phase [6]. However, their availability is regionally limited. Aquifers offer an alternative porous rock structure capable of storing huge amounts of gases and they are available in many regions. However, significant exploration effort is necessary to prove their gas tightness [6]. All porous rock structures require a high share of cushion gas of about 50-67% of the total amount [7]. The storage of hydrogen in such formations can lead to reactions between the gas and the microorganisms and mineral constituents, which can cause deterioration or depletion of the hydrogen and plugging of the microporous pore spaces [8,9].

Salt Caverns are artificially produced caverns in deep salt beds with typical geometric volumes of

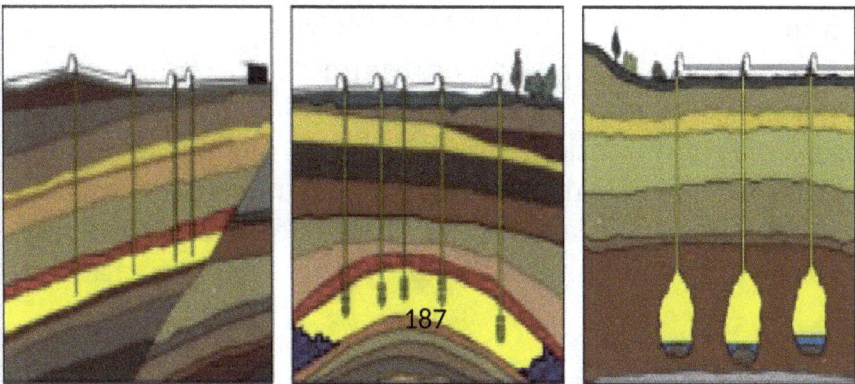

Depleted oil and gas fields   Aquifers   Salt caverns

500,000 m3 and operating pressures between 60 bar and 180 bar [10]. Cushion gas requirements of 20-35% are lower than in porous rock structures [6,7]. The surrounding rock salt is chemically inert to the medium stored, making it suitable for storing hydrogen [8]. The costs for a new cavern measuring 750,000 m3 are estimated to be between £20-30 million [11].

Fig.5 Different underground storage types

3.1.2 Gas distribution

A gas distribution system transports the gas from the supply source to the consumer. In the case of natural gas (NG), most countries have a well-developed infrastructure, connecting the major supply sites with the consumers, which are primarily households, industry and power plants. In Germany, the NG pipeline has a total length of about 524,000 km and is connected to about 50% of all households [12]. The injection of Hydrogen or methane into existing Natural gas grid infrastructure would therefore enable access to established market. However, the maximum allowable concentration of

Hydrogen in the gas mixture must be taken into account as the limiting factor for hydrogen injection. The German Technical and Scientific Association for Gas and Water (DVGW) limits the maximum H2 concentration to 5 vol.% to ensure a standard quality [13]. The technical limitation depends on the individual components, such as the compressors, as well as the end-users.

Pure hydrogen can be transported via trailer in the liquid or gaseous state as well as transport via pipeline. Simulations show that for large amounts of hydrogen, pipeline transport is the most efficient option. However, a dedicated hydrogen pipeline would have to be designed and constructed.

3.2 Applications and end-use technologies

Two major technologies and applications; stationary end-users and use of pure hydrogen in fuel cell

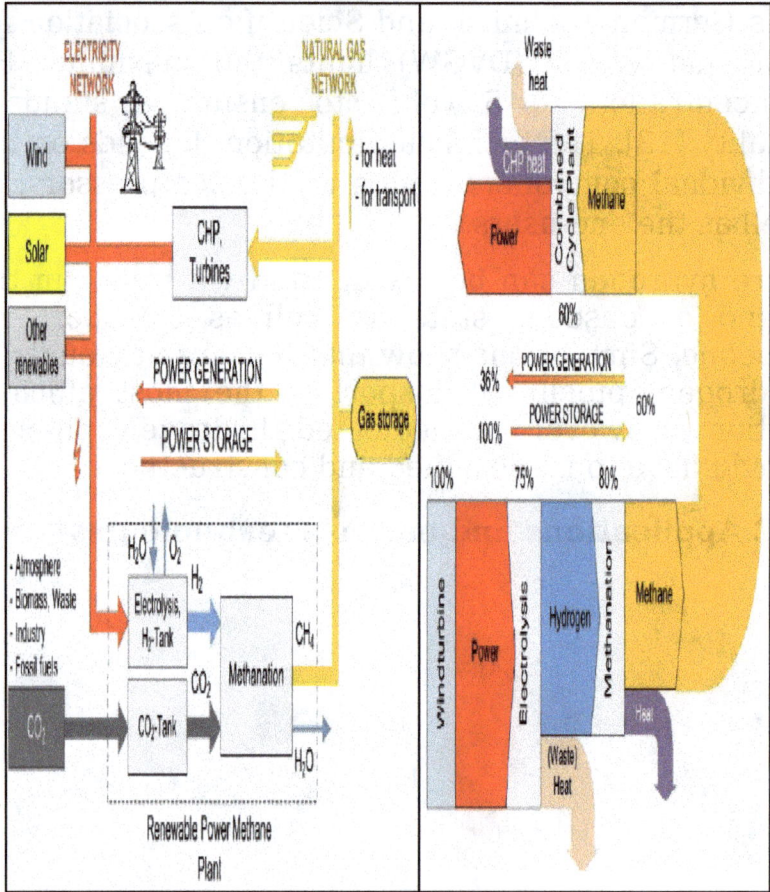

vehicles.

Fig.6. Applications and Energy losses during power to Gas Process

3.2.1 End use in stationary applications

The major applications for natural gas are heating in households, commerce and services, centralized power generation in gas turbines and decentralized combined heat and power plants. Adding hydrogen to natural gas alters the combustion properties, for example, it slightly increases the combustion temperature, reduces ignition delay times and increases the laminar flame speed [14]. Current limitations for gas turbines are 3-4 vol.%H2 [15], but it is estimated that new systems will be able to cope with higher values of about 10-15 vol.%H2 [16]. For residential endues applications, hydrogen contents up to 20 vol.% appear to be no problem [15]

3.2.2 End use in passenger cars

Use of hydrogen and methane can be used to reduce CO_2 emissions in the transportation sector and create energy efficient and low or even zero-emission vehicles. Today, passenger cars with ICEs running on compressed natural gas (CNG) are commercially available. Regarding the admixture of H_2 in CNG, fuel systems and combustion engines are expected to operate reliably with blends up to 30% H_2 [17], but the storage vessels limit the maximum concentration to 2% H_2 [18]. Hence for pure Hydrogen, the focus has been shifted to fuel cell

191

electric vehicles (FCVs). First demonstrations of FCVs show use of 1kg H_2 covers 100km. Current developments focus on further improving the efficiency to about 0.7-0.8 kgH_2 per 100 km, long-term stability and cost reduction. If these efforts are successful, a complete fuel cell power generation system with a power output of 80 kW_{el} and a storage capacity of 5 kg H_2 would cost £4100 [14]

3.2.3 Re-electrification

Re-electrification (Gas to power) can be achieved through fuel cells with efficiencies around 50% or conventional combustion in gas turbines with approximately 55% efficiency in modern closed-cycle gas turbine plants (CCGT), leading to an overall efficiency of about 40 – 45%. Electrification in fuel cells results in water vapor while combustion engines will emit water vapor and small amounts of nitrogen oxides.

Methanation of hydrogen is an optional step once the limit for hydrogen injection in the gas grid has been reached. And the methane (99%) formed can be completely injected into the natural gas grids, making the full 220TWh available in the example of Germany. Re-electrification with methane uses the combine cycle power generation process with a decreased overall efficiency in the range of 30-40%. The bound CO_2 will be emitted again during re-electrification, making the whole process CO_2-neutral.

3.0   Economic Analysis

The comparative study of different storage solutions cannot be done without studying the economic data carefully. For each technology, the investment costs (CAPEX), which may decline in terms of power to energy and operating costs (OPEX) are taken into account. Furthermore, it should reflect the replacement costs (and in fact, alternative frequencies) technologies such as batteries.

In order to compare the relevance of the real costs of storage solutions in regards to Power to Gas (Hydrogen), it is essential to integrate the usual parameters (life, stress frequency, etc.). The emerging nature of the sector and the lack of feedback to submit this analysis still have significant uncertainties. As compared to other storage technologies power to hydrogen is not the most economical but can be used for large energy storage needs.

Furthermore, based on a future power generation structure in Germany, economic analysis was done for three scenarios presented as follows; [3]

Scenario 1, is where hydrogen is directly fed into the natural gas grid, the calculated costs was £0.15/kWh$_{th}$. This cost reveals huge impact of the prices for the electric energy used. Compared to today's natural gas feedstock costs of £0.04/kWh$_{th}$ The cost quadruples.

Scenario 2. Is where hydrogen is converted to methane and fed into the gas grid, the cost increased to £0.23/kWh$_{th}$ due to a reduced efficiency and additional investment costs, making power to gas less attractive as a substitute for natural gas for industry

Scenario 3 is the use of pure hydrogen in the fuel cell electric vehicles. Given already with today's efficiencies of 1 kgH$_2$ per 100 km, hydrogen only costs about 23% more than its range based equivalent in gasoline, which is much more cost efficient than its alternative use as a substitute natural gas. The conclusion that the most economic use for hydrogen is in the transportation sector has also been affirmed by several studies for Germany and the EU [21-23].

4.0   Conclusion

The rising share of fluctuating renewable power production will lead to an increase in required storage capacity in order to provide daily, weekly and seasonal balancing capabilities. The conversion of electric into chemical energy enables largescale storage and the coupling of the different energy markets. In this paper, the core elements of the power-to-gas process chains were presented and their technical feasibility was shown. However, such storage options will only be realizable worldwide if they are economically competitive.

Use of stored hydrogen from water hydrolysis could provide a big possibility for large scale energy storage to generate electricity using Concentrated Solar Power (CSP) in the North African regions in the periods of no sunshine.

When renewable hydrogen or methane is fed into the natural gas grid, the production costs are several times higher than those for conventional natural gas, which renders largescale realization uneconomic.

On the other hand, the utilization of renewable hydrogen in the transportation sector as a fuel for fuel cell electric vehicles has the potential to become an economically sound business case, since the high efficiency of the fuel cell vehicles allows for the cost competiveness of hydrogen compared to gasoline.

Major barriers for this application involve the lack of a hydrogen infrastructure, which must be implemented from scratch. Such a large project can only be successful if the public, politics and industry concur on this matter. It would allow for a cost-effective transition to renewable energy, which would not be limited to the electricity sector but would also include the transportation sector and the chemical industry.

CHAPTER EIGHT

ENERGY KIOSK MODEL

The energy kiosk model is an approach to provide electricity to low income households in off-grid regions. The kiosk produces electricity, usually using a solar panel, and sells it to users through charging devices. A variety of actors – including multi-national companies, start-ups, governmental initiatives, and non-governmental organisations – are engaged in energy kiosk initiatives. Kiosk models can be simple charging stations for lamps and batteries, or multi-service stations offering retail products, entertainment and education. You can find successful showcases especially in Sub-Saharan Africa and India, though only few projects have gone beyond the pilot stage. Although the model works in principle, it seems difficult to create, scale, and replicate projects that have a positive social impact and are economically viable in the long term.

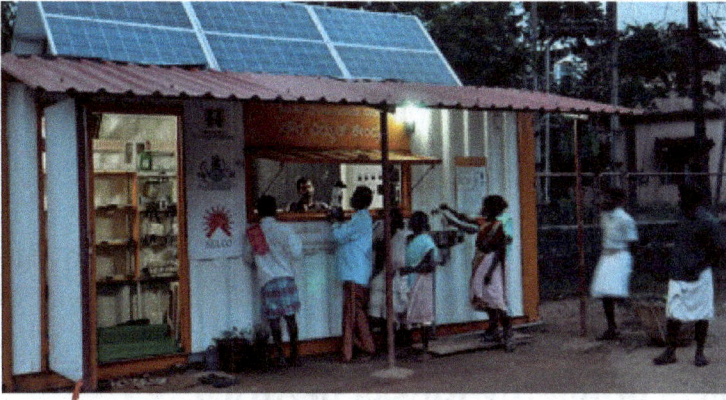

What is an energy kiosk? Energy kiosks are central stations for electricity production and provision to consumers, usually in remote rural areas far off the central grid. In most cases, electricity is produced by solar panels, sometimes complemented by a diesel generator for backup. The electricity reaches consumers through devices with a battery that are charged at the energy kiosk. These devices could be mobile phones, lanterns of different sizes, car batteries or specifically designed battery boxes to plug in razors or radios at home. Most energy kiosks reach less than 100 households with their charging services. A common approach for energy kiosk businesses is the offer of other energy-based services in addition to charging, for example printing and copying services or screenings of football matches. ± Photo: HERi MadagascarEndeva Business Model Library October 2014 The Energy Kiosk Model 06 Introduction In the scope of this research, we only analysed projects that comprise several energy kiosks with a centralised management structure. Small charging stations run by an individual shop owner exist in many villages in off-grid areas, but these initiatives stay local and are not replicated on larger scale. The projects of interest in this Business Model Library issue are multiplying the system on different sites and at scaling up the model to achieve overall profitability.

Prospects of Energy Kiosks in Africa:

Energy kiosks have emerged as a promising solution to address the energy needs of rural and underserved communities in Africa. These kiosks provide access to clean and affordable energy products such as solar lanterns, home systems, and portable stoves. They also serve as charging stations for mobile phones and offer additional services like internet connectivity and health education. While energy kiosks have shown great potential, there are both prospects and challenges that need to be considered

Increased access to electricity: Energy kiosks help bridge the energy access gap by providing communities with reliable and affordable electricity. They enable households to access lighting solutions for activities such as studying, cooking, and socializing, thus improving the quality of life.

Income generation and entrepreneurship: Energy kiosks create income-generating opportunities for entrepreneurs who manage and operate them. These entrepreneurs can earn income through product sales, phone charging services, and other value-added services. This promotes local economic development and supports rural entrepreneurship.

Product customization and affordability: Energy kiosks allow customers to choose energy products and services that suit their needs and budgets. The variety of products available can range from low-cost solar lamps to larger solar home systems. The affordability and flexibility of these products make them accessible to a wide range of consumers.

Environmental sustainability: By providing clean and renewable energy options, energy kiosks contribute to reducing dependence on fossil fuels and mitigating carbon emissions. This helps combat climate change and improves environmental sustainability in the long run.

Challenges of Energy Kiosks in Africa:

Initial investment and infrastructure: Establishing energy kiosks requires significant upfront investment in infrastructure, such as solar panels, batteries, and charging stations. Infrastructure challenges, including limited connectivity and poor roads, can also make it difficult to set up and maintain these kiosks in remote areas.

Affordability and financial sustainability: Ensuring affordability for both the kiosk operators and customers is crucial. Kiosk operators often require financial support or access to funding to set up their businesses. Customers, especially those with limited financial resources, may struggle to afford upfront costs. Sustainable business models that ensure revenue generation and affordable payment plans need to be developed.

Product quality and maintenance: Energy kiosks need to focus on providing high-quality and reliable products to gain the trust of customers. On-going maintenance and repair services are essential to ensure the longevity and effectiveness of energy products.

Smart Solar Kiosk - Burundi and Rwanda

This activity developed a solar-power mobile kiosk to provide access to income-generating opportunities for vulnerable groups such as unemployed youth and women. Smart Solar Kiosk uses renewable energy to produce electricity to charge mobile phones on a business scale.

Fast facts:

- Each solar powered kiosk can charge up to 30 mobile phones and small devices at one time;

- In addition to mobile phone charging, customers can also purchase mobile and solar products and electronic vouchers;
- Each kiosk comes with Wi-Fi internet access;
- As of today, this activity has 25 mobile solar kiosks on the ground in Rwanda and one kiosk in Burundi.

The problem

The national grid in Rwanda services only 17% of the population, so many businesses face electricity shortages, which does not allow them to operate their businesses to full potential.

The solution

With several mobile solar kiosks on the ground, businesses too will have opportunities to charge their mobile phones quickly, cheaply, cleanly and with flexibility. This activity has developed a low-cost franchise business model that enables entrepreneurial-minded individuals that are otherwise financially excluded to deliver services and products at competitive prices, thereby generating rapid revenue growth and fostering income growth. Kiosks are equipped with charging stations powered to charge small electronic devices through solar energy and offer services and products ranging from mobile money transfers, electronic vouchers and Wi-Fi access.

Helping the planet

Smart Solar Kiosks replace fossil fuels with solar energy, thus reducing carbon emissions.

Helping people

This activity has created a platform for women to start their own Smart Solar Kiosk franchises. Women wanting to open their own franchise will require less investment to start a franchise. This activity is also working with youth and disabilities. They are locating funding opportunities for them to finance their business.

Scaling Up

This activity aims to develop partnerships with major telecommunication companies in the region, which can provide more services at more economical prices. This will help franchises sell a wider selection of products and services to their customers, thus increasing their revenues. Smart Solar Kiosks also hopes to expand to other African countries by developing local partnerships with distributors and franchises.

List of Bibliography

Ajaz, W. & Bernell, D. (2021). Microgrids and the transition toward decentralized energy systems in the United States: A Multi-Level Perspective. Energy Policy. oregonstate.edu

Al-Shetwi, A. Q. (2022). Sustainable development of renewable energy integrated power sector: Trends, environmental impacts, and recent challenges. Science of The Total Environment. [HTML]

Angelus, A. (2021). Distributed renewable power generation and implications for capacity investment and electricity prices. Production and Operations Management. [HTML]

Anser, M. K., Usman, M., Sharif, M., Bashir, S., Shabbir, M. S., Yahya Khan, G., & Lopez, L. B. (2022). The dynamic impact of renewable energy sources on environmental economic growth: evidence from selected Asian economies. Environmental Science and Pollution Research, 29(3), 3323-3335. uca.es

Bakay, M. S. & Ağbulut, Ü (2021). Electricity production based forecasting of greenhouse gas emissions in Turkey with deep learning, support vector machine and artificial neural network algorithms. Journal of Cleaner Production. [HTML]

Bangjun, W., Feng, Z., Feng, J., Yu, P., & Cui, L. (2022). Decision making on investments in photovoltaic power generation projects based on renewable portfolio standard: Perspective of real option. Renewable Energy. [HTML]

Bhuiyan, M. R. A. (2022). Overcome the future environmental challenges through sustainable and renewable energy resources. Micro & Nano Letters. wiley.com

Bianco, V., Cascetta, F., & Nardini, S. (2021). Analysis of technology diffusion policies for renewable energy. The case of the Italian solar photovoltaic sector. Sustainable Energy Technologies and Assessments, 46, 101250. [HTML]

Butters, R. A., Dorsey, J., & Gowrisankaran, G. (2021). Soaking up the sun: Battery investment, renewable energy, and market equilibrium. nber.org

Chen, Y., Jensen, I. G., Kirkerud, J. G., & Bolkesjø, T. F. (2021). Impact of fossil-free decentralized heating on northern European renewable energy deployment and the power system. Energy. sciencedirect.com

Cohen, J. J., Azarova, V., Kollmann, A., & Reichl, J. (2021). Preferences for community renewable energy investments in Europe. Energy Economics. sciencedirect.com

Crippa, M., Solazzo, E., Guizzardi, D., Monforti-Ferrario, F., Tubiello, F. N., & Leip, A. J. N. F. (2021). Food systems are responsible for a third of global anthropogenic GHG emissions. Nature food, 2(3), 198-209. ed.ac.uk

de Castro, C. & Capellán-Pérez, I. (2020). ... of use, and extended energy return on energy invested (EROI) from comprehensive material requirements of present global wind, solar, and hydro power technologies. Energies. mdpi.com

Fang, K., Li, C., Tang, Y., He, J., & Song, J. (2022). China's pathways to peak carbon emissions: New insights from various industrial sectors. Applied Energy. zju.edu.cn

Grabara, J., Tleppayev, A., Dabylova, M., Mihardjo, L. W., & Dacko-Pikiewicz, Z. (2021). Empirical research on the relationship amongst renewable energy consumption, economic growth and foreign direct investment in Kazakhstan and Uzbekistan. Energies, 14(2), 332. mdpi.com

Handayani, K., Anugrah, P., Goembira, F., Overland, I., Suryadi, B., & Swandaru, A. (2022). Moving beyond the NDCs: ASEAN pathways to a net-zero emissions power sector in 2050. Applied Energy, 311, 118580. sciencedirect.com

Hannan, M. A., Al-Shetwi, A. Q., Ker, P. J., Begum, R. A., Mansor, M., Rahman, S. A., ... & Muttaqi, K. M. (2021). Impact of renewable energy utilization and artificial intelligence in achieving sustainable development goals. Energy Reports, 7, 5359-5373. sciencedirect.com

Hao, F. & Shao, W. (2021). What really drives the deployment of renewable energy? A global assessment of 118 countries. Energy Research & Social Science. [HTML]

Heldeweg, M. A. & Saintier, S. (2020). Renewable energy communities as 'socio-legal institutions': A normative frame for energy decentralization?.

Renewable and Sustainable Energy Reviews. sciencedirect.com

Hong, C., Burney, J. A., Pongratz, J., Nabel, J. E., Mueller, N. D., Jackson, R. B., & Davis, S. J. (2021). Global and regional drivers of land-use emissions in 1961–2017. Nature, 589(7843), 554-561. nsf.gov

Ibekwe, K. I., Ohenhen, P. E., Chidolue, O., Umoh, A. A., Ngozichukwu, B., Ilojianya, V. I., & Fafure, A. V. (2024). Microgrid systems in US energy infrastructure: A comprehensive review: Exploring decentralized energy solutions, their benefits, and challenges in regional implementation. World Journal of Advanced Research and Reviews, 21(1), 973-987. wjarr.com

Javid, I., Chauhan, A., Thappa, S., Verma, S. K., Anand, Y., Sawhney, A., ... & Anand, S. (2021). Futuristic decentralized clean energy networks in view of inclusive-economic growth and sustainable society. Journal of Cleaner Production, 309, 127304. [HTML]

Kabeyi, M. J. B. & Olanrewaju, O. A. (2022). Sustainable energy transition for renewable and low carbon grid electricity generation and supply. Frontiers in Energy research. frontiersin.org

Khan, S. A. R., Zhang, Y., Kumar, A., Zavadskas, E., & Streimikiene, D. (2020). Measuring the impact of renewable energy, public health expenditure, logistics, and environmental performance on sustainable economic growth. Sustainable development, 28(4), 833-843. vilniustech.lt

Kök, A. G., Shang, K., & Yücel, Ş. (2020). Investments in renewable and conventional energy: The role of operational flexibility. Manufacturing & Service Operations Management, 22(5), 925-941. utoronto.ca

Kumar, M. (2020). Social, economic, and environmental impacts of renewable energy resources. Wind solar hybrid renewable energy system. intechopen.com

Levenda, A. M., Behrsin, I., & Disano, F. (2021). Renewable energy for whom? A global systematic review of the environmental justice implications of renewable energy technologies. Energy Research & Social Science. [HTML]

Li, L. & Zhang, S. (2021). Techno-economic and environmental assessment of multiple distributed energy systems coordination under centralized and decentralized framework. Sustainable Cities and Society. [HTML]

Li, R., Wang, X., & Wang, Q. (2022). Does renewable energy reduce ecological footprint at the expense of economic growth? An empirical analysis of 120 countries. Journal of Cleaner Production. [HTML]

Madeddu, S., Ueckerdt, F., Pehl, M., Peterseim, J., Lord, M., Kumar, K. A., ... & Luderer, G. (2020). The CO2 reduction potential for the European industry via direct electrification of heat supply (power-to-heat). Environmental Research Letters, 15(12), 124004. iop.org

Meju, M. A. & Saleh, A. S. (2023). Using Large-Size Three-Dimensional Marine Electromagnetic Data for the Efficient Combined Investigation of Natural Hydrogen and Hydrocarbon Gas Reservoirs: A .... Minerals. mdpi.com

Moriarty, P. & Honnery, D. (2022). Renewable energy in an increasingly uncertain future. Applied Sciences. mdpi.com

Nassar, Y. F., Salem, M. A., Iessa, K. R., AlShareef, I. M., Ali, K. A., & Fakher, M. A. (2021). Estimation of CO_2 emission factor for the energy industry sector in Libya: A case study. Environment, Development and Sustainability, 23, 13998-14026. researchgate.net

Niekurzak, M. (2021). The potential of using renewable energy sources in Poland taking into account the economic and ecological conditions. Energies. mdpi.com

Nong, D., Simshauser, P., & Nguyen, D. B. (2021). Greenhouse gas emissions vs CO2 emissions: Comparative analysis of a global carbon tax. Applied Energy. sciencedirect.com

Nsafon, B. E. K., Owolabi, A. B., Butu, H. M., Roh, J. W., Suh, D., & Huh, J. S. (2020). Optimization and sustainability analysis of PV/wind/diesel hybrid energy system for decentralized energy generation. Energy Strategy Reviews, 32, 100570. sciencedirect.com

Østergaard, P. A., Duic, N., Noorollahi, Y., & Kalogirou, S. (2020). Latest progress in Sustainable Development using renewable energy technology. Renewable energy. [HTML]

Özkan, O., Alola, A. A., & Eluwole, K. K. (2024). Dynamic environmental quality effect of nuclear energy intensity, structural changes, and natural resources in Pakistan: testing load capacity factor hypothesis evidence. Environment, Development and Sustainability, 1-18. springer.com

Pradhan, S., Ghose, D., & Shabbiruddin. (2020). Present and future impact of COVID-19 in the renewable energy sector: A case study on India. Energy Sources, Part A: Recovery, Utilization, and Environmental Effects, 1-11. [HTML]

Qu, F., Chen, Y., & Zheng, B. (2021). Is new energy driven by crude oil, high-tech sector or low-carbon notion? New evidence from high-frequency data. Energy. [HTML]

Saçık, S. Y., Yokuş, N., Alagöz, M., & Yokuş, T. (2020). Optimum renewable energy investment planning in terms of current deficit: Turkey model. Energies. mdpi.com

Saidi, K. & Omri, A. (2020). The impact of renewable energy on carbon emissions and economic growth in

15 major renewable energy-consuming countries. Environmental research. [HTML]

Sayed, E. T., Wilberforce, T., Elsaid, K., Rabaia, M. K. H., Abdelkareem, M. A., Chae, K. J., & Olabi, A. G. (2021). A critical review on environmental impacts of renewable energy systems and mitigation strategies: Wind, hydro, biomass and geothermal. Science of the total environment, 766, 144505. [HTML]

SIDHARTH, D. R. G. (). Trading in Solar Renewable Energy Certificates by the Households: An Underutilized Potential in India. researchgate.net. researchgate.net

Soltani, M., Kashkooli, F. M., Souri, M., Rafiei, B., Jabarifar, M., Gharali, K., & Nathwani, J. S. (2021). Environmental, economic, and social impacts of geothermal energy systems. Renewable and Sustainable Energy Reviews, 140, 110750. [HTML]

Stoddard, I., Anderson, K., Capstick, S., Carton, W., Depledge, J., Facer, K., ... & Williams, M. (2021). Three decades of climate mitigation: why haven't we bent the global emissions curve?. Annual Review of Environment and Resources, 46(1), 653-689. annualreviews.org

Sun, Y., Guan, W., Razzaq, A., Shahzad, M., & An, N. B. (2022). Transition towards ecological sustainability through fiscal decentralization, renewable energy and green investment in OECD countries. Renewable Energy. [HTML]

Taubner, R. S., Olsson-Francis, K., Vance, S. D., Ramkissoon, N. K., Postberg, F., de Vera, J. P., ... & Soderlund, K. M. (2020). Experimental and simulation efforts in the astrobiological exploration of exooceans. Space Science Reviews, 216, 1-41. springer.com

Voldsgaard, A. (2023). Analysing Renewable Energy Finance as an Evolving Complex System: Lessons from Offshore Wind. ucl.ac.uk

Wang, K. H., Su, C. W., Lobonț, O. R., & Moldovan, N. C. (2020). Chinese renewable energy industries' boom and recession: Evidence from bubble detection procedure. Energy Policy. [HTML]

Wang, Q., Dong, Z., Li, R., & Wang, L. (2022). Renewable energy and economic growth: New insight from country risks. Energy. e-tarjome.com

Wen, J., Okolo, C. V., Ugwuoke, I. C., & Kolani, K. (2022). Research on influencing factors of renewable energy, energy efficiency, on technological innovation. Does trade, investment and human capital development matter?. Energy Policy. [HTML]

Wisian, K. & Boul, P. (2023). Other Strategic Considerations for Geothermal in Texas in The Future of Geothermal in Texas: Contemporary Prospects and Perspectives. utexas.edu

Wu, Z., Njoke, M. L., Tian, G., & Feng, J. (2021). Challenges of investment and financing for developing photovoltaic power generation in Cameroon, and the countermeasures. Journal of Cleaner Production. [HTML]

Yeilding, C. A., Sears, R. A., Donovan, Z. M., & Hernández-Molina, F. J. (2022). Deepwater sedimentary systems: The next 100 years of deepwater. In Deepwater Sedimentary Systems (pp. 723-754). Elsevier. [HTML]

Yiming, W., Xun, L., Umair, M., & Aizhan, A. (2024). COVID-19 and the transformation of emerging economies: Financialization, green bonds, and stock market volatility. Resources Policy. [HTML]

Zhao, Y., Yuan, H., Zhang, Z., & Gao, Q. (2024). Performance analysis and multi-objective optimization of the offshore renewable energy powered integrated energy supply system. Energy Conversion and Management. [HTML]

Zhou, P., Luo, J., Cheng, F., Yüksel, S., & Dinçer, H. (2021). Analysis of risk priorities for renewable energy investment projects using a hybrid IT2 hesitant fuzzy decision-making approach with alpha cuts. Energy. [HTML]

Zhou, S., Tong, Q., Pan, X., Cao, M., Wang, H., Gao, J., & Ou, X. (2021). Research on low-carbon energy transformation of China necessary to achieve the Paris agreement goals: A global perspective. Energy Economics. [HTML]

Mmap Nonfiction and Academic books

If you have enjoyed **ENERGY KIOSK** , consider these other fine **Mmap Nonfiction and Academic books** from *Mwanaka Media and Publishing:*

Cultural Hybridity and Fixity by Andrew Nyongesa

Tintinnabulation of Literary Theory by Andrew Nyongesa

South Africa and United Nations Peacekeeping Offensive Operations by Antonio Garcia

A Case of Love and Hate by Chenjerai Mhondera

A Cat and Mouse Affair by Bruno Shora

The Scholarship Girl by Abigail George

The Gods Sleep Through It All by Wonder Guchu

PHENOMENOLOGY OF DECOLONIZING THE UNIVERSITY: Essays in the Contemporary Thoughts of Afrikology by Zvikomborero Kapuya

Africanization and Americanization Anthology Volume 1, Searching for Interracial, Interstitial, Intersectional and Interstates Meeting Spaces, Africa Vs North America by Tendai R Mwanaka

Africa, UK and Ireland: Writing Politics and Knowledge Production Vol 1 by Tendai R Mwanaka

Writing Language, Culture and Development, Africa Vs Asia Vol 1 by Tendai R Mwanaka, Wanjohi wa Makokha and Upal Deb

Zimbolicious: An Anthology of Zimbabwean Literature and Arts, Vol 3 by Tendai Mwanaka

Drawing Without Licence by Tendai R Mwanaka

Writing Grandmothers/ Escribiendo sobre nuestras raíces: Africa Vs Latin America Vol 2 by Tendai R Mwanaka and Felix Rodriguez

Nationalism: (Mis)Understanding Donald Trump's Capitalism, Racism, Global Politics, International Trade and Media Wars, Africa Vs North America Vol 2 by Tendai R Mwanaka

It Is Not About Me: Diaries 2010-2011 by Tendai Rinos Mwanaka

Chitungwiza Mushamukuru: An Anthology from Zimbabwe's Biggest Ghetto Town by Tendai Rinos Mwanaka

The Day and the Dweller: A Study of the Emerald Tablets by Jonathan Thompson

Zimbolicious Anthology Vol 4: An Anthology of Zimbabwean Literature and Arts by Tendai Rinos Mwanaka and Jabulani Mzinyathi

Parks and Recreation by Abigail George

FAMILY LAW AND POLITICS WITH BIOLOGY AND ROYALTY IN AFRICA AND NORTH AMERICA by Peter Ateh-Afec Fossungu

Writing Robotics, Africa Vs Asia, Vol 2 by Tendai Rinos Mwanaka

Zimbolicious Anthology Vol 5: An Anthology of Zimbabwean Literature and Arts by Tendai R. Mwanaka

Love Notes: Everything is Love, An Anthology of Indigenous Languages of Africa and East Europe by Tendai R Mwanaka

Zimbolicious Anthology Vol 6: An Anthology of Zimbabwean Literature and Arts by Tendai R. Mwanaka and Chenjerai Mhondera

BATTLING LANGUAGE RIGHTS GOVERNANCE IN AFRICA: SWISSELGIANISM, UBACKISM, AND THE AMBAZONIA-CAMEROUN WAR by Peter Ateh-Afec Fossungu

Otherness and Pathology: The Fragmented Self and Madness in Contemporary African Fiction by Andrew Nyongesa

Zimbabwe: The Urgency of Now by Tendai Rinos Mwanaka

Zimbabwe: The Blame Game, Recollected essays and Non-fictions by Tendai Rinos Mwanaka

The Trick is to Keep Breathing: Covid 19 Stories From African and North American Writers, Vol 3 by Tendai Rinos Mwanaka

Recentring Mother Earth by Andrew Nyongesa

VENI VIDI VICI AND LAND GRABBING by Nkwazi Mhango

I Can't Breathe and other Essays by Zvikomborero Kapuya

Ayabacholization Classroom In My Life: The Longest Shortcut To University Education by Peter Ateh-Afec Fossungu

Gathering Evidence by Tendai Rinos Mwanaka

Best New African poets 10th anniversary: Interviews and   Reviews by Tendai Rinos Mwanaka

In the footsteps of a Bipolar Life by Ambrose Cato George and Abigail George

No Business Like Love Business by Peter Atec-Afec Fossungu

Upcoming books

Manifestations of trauma in the post-2000 Zimbabwean Literature by Nyarai Maria Kanyemba

https://facebook.com/MwanakaMediaAndPublishing

www.ingramcontent.com/pod-product-compliance
Lightning Source LLC
Chambersburg PA
CBHW070326270326
41926CB00017B/3777